Financial Freedom

The Best Path To Accelerate Your Journey To Retirement Through Passive Income And Real Estate Business

Timothy Turner

PART 1:

Passive Income

A Complete Step-by-Step Guide to Building Multiple Streams of Income and Finally Gain Freedom and Financial Independence

Timothy Turner

Table of Contents

Prologue

"Making money while you sleep."

It sounds good, doesn't it? This is the desire of many people and some have succeeded in earning passive income from several streams. If your goal is to earn money while you sleep, you have to reach a certain point where every asset you own will earn money for you. However, to reach this point is not as easy as it sounds. You will need to dedicate money, time, and work. Passive income is defined as the process where money is earned with little activity when compared to a full time job through a number of ventures that demand little upkeep or daily effort on the person's part.

You will be able to earn passive income whether you are someone who has extra money you want to invest or an entrepreneur with an amazing business plan. On the most basic level, you will be able to earn money through passive income opportunities with considerably less effort, but you should bear in mind that the term can be a bit deceptive because this type of income is not completely passive. Becoming an expert of generating passive income does not mean that you will do nothing and only watch the cash rolling in. If your goal is money with no effort, you will most probably get scammed or take a very dangerous risk of facing a bad situation.

Passive income can result in you having more free time, but in order for you to get to this point you will have to work, sometimes hard because it may take a lot of hustle depending on the different passive income ideas you will want to follow. This amount of work will become less or at least remain the same once the business is ready while your gains will continue to increase.

One other thing you should keep in mind is that passive income will take time to develop. You may think about pursuing this type of hustle, as many do, but you are not taking any action like most people. Most of those people will be stuck on the analysis stage and never actually take that extremely important step to their financial freedom. Your first days, after you decide to take this step and earn passive income, will be dedicated to educating yourself on finance, business, and investments.

Do not try to learn everything there is out there because they will never be enough and will only confuse you. In other words, do not be afraid to fail. You will see that those extremely successful people will tell you that their failures are what allowed them to be where they are today. Anybody can do it. Anybody can start earning passive income and reach a point where he or she has achieved financial freedom. Let us see how through this complete guide of how to earn passive income.

In the first chapter, we will present you with the different streams of income and mainly the ones successful people use to better understand later the gist of passive income. In the second chapter, we will introduce you to robo advisors which are a great way for you to invest your money without the hustle of having to build and manage your investment portfolio. Let the robo advisors do those things for you.

In the third chapter, we will present you the different ways you can build your wealth through passive real estate investing. Passive real estate investing is a great way to multiply your money without having to deal with the various problems and stress an active investor has to go through with investment properties. In the fourth chapter, we will show you another great stream of passive income that is opening and maintaining a high-yield savings account. This stream of passive income is often characterized as the simplest, safest, and most boring investment that was ever created and this may have some truth in it. Let us see in the fourth chapter why.

 In the fifth chapter, we will present you with the various things you need to know in order to invest in certificates of deposit. This stream of passive income has many benefits, but if you need immediate access to your money, this is not the best choice for you. They usually have a time frame during which you will not be able to touch them. However, they also perfect for accumulating your money if you can get passed through this little drawback. More about this passive income option, in chapter five.

In the sixth chapter, we will show you all the things you need to consider and plan when you decide to earn a considerable amount of passive income through Airbnb©. This is a great option that you can later turn into a full business by dedicating more of your time to plan things though. Let's find more about this great passive income option in chapter six. In the seventh chapter, we will show you the last effective way for you to be able to earn the passive income that could set you on the right track of gaining your financial freedom. This las source of passive income is Index Funds. Let us learn more about them in the seventh and final chapter.

The Different Streams of Income

Usually, people are making money from one source of income or two. However, did you know that there are different streams of income you can start making money off? Streams of income that even millionaires apply? There are more on how to earn money that you probably know of. The internet is filled with books and articles on how to get rich quickly and be a millionaire overnight, but most people are not aware of the different ways they will be able to earn more money and live comfortably or are simply too afraid of the risks involved and do nothing about it. It may be also the fact that some people do not want to make millions of dollars in a few years, but they wish to reduce the time they spend each day on making money from their main source of income, which is their full-time job.

Typically, there are three ways to be able to earn money:

Capital gains:

Usually, when we refer to capital gains we talk about an underlying asset that has risen in value and then sold for profit. A capital asset is almost every personal item you own such as investments, a car, or real estate. However, if you own a business, the assets of your business are not capital assets including supplies for business purposes, equipment, and inventory. Also, capital assets are not any songs you have produced or the copyrights to your creations. There is a simple investing concept that has to do with selling high and buying low.

If you have sold anything including a car, a house, stocks, gold coins, you most probably have a capital loss or gain. When compared to a standard salary, capital gains are taxed with a more favorable rate and this is the reason why this income stream is considered to have a greater effect on your pocket. However, not all capital gains are the same and there are some exceptions to the above fact. The tax rate of a capital gain is based on the two categories of capital gain, which are the following:

✓ Short-term capital gain
✓ Long-term capital gain

When we refer to short-term capital gains, we include profits that come from the sale of an asset you had ownership for approximately a year or less. This capital gain does not have the benefits of a special tax rate since it is taxed as your salary does. The exact opposite is long-term capital gain. If you own this asset form more than a year, you will benefit from a less tax rate on your gains. These two categories were created to enhance long-term investments in the economy.

Labour:

The most common and essential way of making money is labor, a process where your time is exchanged for money. Earned income, which is one of the various streams of income is considered to be the money you earn through spending your time on it, for instance through working for someone. This is the part where your quality of life will be endangered to suffer the most since you will trade valuable time for money. Most jobs will pay enough for you to not be broke.

The most common reason why people are not able to move on from making money through their job is that it offers them a comfort zone. Unfortunately, this comfort zone is a double-edged knife and can become your biggest enemy since it will keep you from having an amazing life. In other words, you will spend most of your life earning money only from this income stream and you will not have enough money to be wealthy and have a comfortable life. To quote the words from the Rat Race to Financial Freedom:

"Comfort is your biggest trap and coming out of comfort zone your biggest enemy"

Passive income:

Your asset will generate income, but its value is not altered when the revenues are generated. You will know how much you make from passive income from the difference between the income and the expenses needed when you manage the asset.

Profit Income:

Through profit income, you earn money from selling a product for more than it costed you to make. For example, shirts, laptops, mobile phones, no matter if you are at the retail or on a wholesale level. To earn profits you have to be an entrepreneur. To start a business, you will probably need a huge investment or begin with a small business for profit with a small investment. However, you should keep in mind that this will require a lot of your time, especially through your first steps, until you are able to manage your business very well and let make money on its own.

Being an entrepreneur demands a different type of mindset as well as the capability of taking risks. Most people in a job are used to the stream of earning income and wish to make the move towards this category at a certain stage of their careers. However, they find it very difficult to make this move, because they are afraid of the added risks. This fear is often justified due to the constraints many people have on their needs and due to family reasons.

We will analyze in later chapters what an entrepreneur is, but generally, you will have to make a product or sell a service and manage both your clients and sells very well. Most people think that the only viable tools through which they can earn money are the streams of Earned Income and Profit Income. However, they don't know or forget that there are more serious and reliable ways to generate your wealth.

Interest Income:

When you lend your money to someone else, for example, placing them in a bank or lending them to the government by buying Treasury Bills, you earn money from the stream of Interest Income. This is also one of the top choices of passive income, where no active involvement is necessary once you make the investment. Many people do not understand the amount of wealth they will be able to generate with the Interest Income stream, but when it is linked with compound interest and the fact that it is a passive income with practically no serious risks, it can be better than the two sources of income we mentioned before.

Compound interest is the interest that is added to the initial sum of money, which includes the accumulated interest of all the previous periods of a loan or a deposit. According to Warren Buffet:

"My wealth has come from a combination of living in America, some lucky genes, and compound interest."

Let us take a closer look at how compound interest works. Let's say that you have a mortgage of $20.000 to be paid in 30 years and your interest is 5%. The principal and interest payment will be $1.073,64 and for this amount of money, you will be making 360 payments. On your first payment of this amount, only $240,31 will go to pay the principal amount and $833,33 will go to the interest. As months pass, a few more money will go for the payment of the principal amount of money to slowly bring down the amount. If you calculate all the payments, which are 360 x $1.073,64, the money you will pay will be a total of

$386.510,40 when the 30 year period is over. In other words, the interest you paid was $186.510,40.

If you could take $200.000 and simply divided this amount to 360 payments, you would have to pay each month $555,55. From this example, you see how interest can cause us harm when it works against us. Let us see an example where interest is working for you by using the same amount of $200.000, the same payment scheme with 360 monthly payments with 5% interest, and the same period of 30 years.

If for 30 years you were able to put $1.073,64 each month in an interest-bearing account and earn a 5% interest, at the end of the 30 years you would have $902.066. If the interest was higher at 8%, in thirty years you will have $1.622.517. Albert Einstein knew that compound interest can change lives. In his words:

"Compound interest is the eighth wonder of the world. He who understands it, earns it. He who doesn't, pays it."

Dividend Income:

This stream of income has the potential to be better than Interest Income. It is also considered to be a passive income and it will make you a shareholder of a company.

Through this income stream, you will be able to earn money as a return of the company shares you will own. The dividend is announced by most companies when the year ends. Even though it sounds very good, this is one of the most neglected source of income. If you are able to make a good investment on the ex-dividend dates of companies, the returns from Dividend Income will surpass the ones of Interest Income due to the fact that you will also be a member of the Capital Gains the share price will go through.

To better understand the concept of dividend income, it refers to the distribution of the earnings a company has to its shareholders from mutual funds or stocks that you own. All companies are able to choose several things to do with the earnings they generate. For instance, they are able to keep their earning within their business in order to broaden their operations, accumulate wealth, or pay off their debts. They can also buy shares with their profits or distribute a part of their profits to their shareholders in stock or cash, something that is defined as dividend. Most companies that choose this payment method do so quarterly, however, monthly or annual dividends are not unusual.

If you decide to pursue this stream of income, you will come across the term "qualified dividend". In order for you to be qualified for a low tax rate, the dividend you receive must:

- ✓ Have been paid by a qualified foreign corporation or have been paid by a United States corporation.
- ✓ Have the stock for more than 60 days during a period of 121 days starting 60 days prior to the ex-dividend date. A preferred stock requires to hold it for 90 days out of a period of 181 days, starting 90 days prior to the ex-dividend date of the stock.

Some examples of dividends that are not deemed as "qualified dividends" are money given from when a company sells its property or else capital gain distributions, dividends paid on credit union and bank deposits, dividends from an organization that is exempt from tax, and particular pass-through dividends.

Rental Income:

Another stream of income is the rental income which is money you receive as a result of your renting an asset that you own such as a building or a house. This stream of income is also considered better than the other 4 types we mentioned before, however, it has some drawbacks when compared to the other streams we analyzed.

For instance, this type of investment requires a larger amount of money to make such an asset that will offer you a regular, monthly, rental income. Since the amount of money you will have to invest is huge, you may not be able to creat many assets throughout your life, unless you have other ways to generate income.

When you compare it to the other streams of income, it will be easy to earn Dividend Income or Interest Income with an investment of the amount INR 1.000; however, you will not be able to earn Rental Income with such small amount of cash invested. Another important drawback of this stream is the illiquidity of your assets. If you decide to rearrange your portfolio, it may be difficult for you to liquefy you assets quickly and will need a lot of planning to do so.

Royalty Income:

Through this stream of income, you will earn money resulting from allowing someone to use your ideas, processes, or products. The ones who use your product will do all the hard work and the revenues with you getting a small percentage of whatever money they earn. For example, if you have a shop under the name of a franchise, you will pay royalties to the franchise for using their marketing, their processes, their logo, etc. This is royalty income for their part. If you are an author, you will be paid for every book you sell.

This stream of income has its challenges too. The biggest one is creating something that is unique and then, be able to repeat it. Special skills may be required for the asset you create, but once it is out there, you will have no limit to the amount of money you will earn.

Those were the most common sources of income that are used by millionaires. The truth of the matter is that not all millionaires use all of these streams. In fact, Warren Buffet, who is a billionaire, uses Capital Gains and Dividend Income. However, he did not earn Capital Gains on everything there is, he specialized in Capital Gains of stock market companies. He developed his skills that had to do with valuing and investing in companies. This way he was able to be a millionaire and then turn into a billionaire.

Another example of famous people that managed to accumulate wealth through multiple streams of income is Bill Gates. He was able to generate his income through

Royalty Income and Profit Income streams. Bill Gates founded a company and came up with an asset that we know today as "Windows". Then, he used this asset to completely change the way we work with computers.

The bottom line is that you should focus on how you will be able to make money from these income streams. Then, you can be the best, by developing your skills, in a small part of the particular income streams you created. You should also keep in mind that if you search for people that became millionaires through the Earned income stream, you will find very few. This happens because this is the stream where out time is used least efficiently, and there are limits to the hours we are able to spend there each day.

There is also the limit of the amount of money we will be able to earn from this type of stream. All the other streams of income we analyzed are not entirely dependent on the time we place in them and thus we are able to dedicate as many hours as we wish to become better, accumulate wealth, and achieve financial freedom. Let us move on to the various ways we will be able to turn this into reality.

Robo- Investing

If you are a full-time investor or you are just making your first steps in investing, robo advisors will offer you the chance to automate investing if you wish. Robo advisors will build a fully diversified portfolio based on the preferences of investors, for this reason, they are called automated investment services.

Essentially, they are investment tools that use computer software and algorithms to manage and create an investor's portfolio. This is achieved through a questionnaire given to an investor to conclude your risk tolerance, investment preferences, and investment goals. Then, the robo advisor will offer you the right portfolio, based on your answers, to buy. When this step is complete, the robo advisor will automatically build a diversified investment portfolio as well as choose the funds on your behalf.

This way of managing your investments is a relatively low-cost method that places your portfolio on autopilot. Generally, investors are able to manage and build their portfolio with the following ways:

- ✓ They hire a financial advisor to make a curated portfolio
- ✓ They pick investments themselves
- ✓ They use a robo advisor to make their portfolio

With robo advisors, you will replace the job of a financial advisor and gain the time you will spend by choosing to build a portfolio yourself. This way you will be able to dedicate the time you freed into creating other sources of passive income. You will have to open a robo manager account and then answer the questions you will be given through the online questionnaire. Once you invest your funds, your portfolio will be rearranged to meet the target allocation. Some of the robo advisors offer particular securities when it comes to tax-loss harvesting which will help you lessen the amount of money you will have to pay on taxes.

The different types of investors that can benefit from using robo advisors are the following:

- ✓ Beginner Investors: Such investors do not yet have the necessary financial knowledge to proceed in well-informed investment decisions and are comfortable with letting the management of their portfolio to online services with less human assistance or no human assistance at all.

✓ Professional Investors: Such investors may wish to place their portfolio on automatic pilot since they may not have the time to manage it themselves because they are chasing after other sources of passive income or their portfolio is too big to manage.

✓ Investors that Follow Simple Strategies: A simple strategy for the allocation of your assets may be 60% for stocks and 40% for bonds. These strategies do not require the assistance of a financial advisor who will continuously rebalance your account.

✓ Investors with a Do-It-Yourself Approach: If you don't want to hire a financial advisor and wish to have more free time from having to choose the investments you make on your own, you will be able to get help from a robo advisor to select your investments for you, place trades on your account, and rebalance them.

However, the solution of automated management of your investment portfolio is not ideal for the following types of investors:

✓ Investors who want Human Assistance: Even though there are some robo advisors who will offer you human assistance with the additional costs, you will interact with them through the internet. If you seek someone who you will be able to meet with, in person and stay with you for a long time, robo advisor is not the one to choose.

✓ Investors who Have Many Investment Accounts: If you are an investor that has to manage benefit packages of your company as well as manage many different accounts, this automation process of robo advisor is not suitable for your needs.

✓ Investors that Require a Tailored Management: You will not be able to get customized advice or plans on how much money you will have to save or whether you should use a Traditional IRA or a Roth IRA.

By using an algorithm for your investments, you will get passive income from investing from the comfort of your home, and essentially you will have the time to create other streams of income while you let a computer take care of this part of your passive income plan. There are other benefits of using a robo advisor aside from the automated process that makes investing fall into the category of passive income.

For instance, you will avoid making crucial mistakes. It is a fact that there have been many cases of investors that fail or get very poor outcomes from their investments due to mistakes that have to do with their behavior and mindset. Investors are humans and as humans, we tend to make emotional decisions based on our instincts. Robo advisor software will not make those mistakes.

Also, through the automated process, the software of the robo advisor will take care of all the investment process. You will not have to worry about altering your portfolio or invest less or more money based on the market factor. You will not even be required to enter your account to place trades. Another thing to consider is that you will be able to make smaller investments at a lower cost. Financial advisor firms will typically ask for a higher amount of money from the investor to invest at the beginning and incur fees that can be higher when compared to those that robo advisors charge. You will also not have to worry if the investing recommendation the broker makes is appropriate for you.

When it comes to the fees the robo advisor will charge you, typically, you will have to pay a service fee that can be settled through a percentage of the assets or through a fixed monthly fee that varies from $15 to $200 per month and it depends on the value of your portfolio. If the payment is done through percentages of the assets you may see fees of approximately 0.15% to 0.50% based on the value of your account for each year. For example, if your account is worth $100.000, a 0.15% fee will be translated to $500 per year.

You will also have to pay for any expenses that are linked with investments that are used by the robo advisors. For instance, exchange-traded funds, as well as mutual funds, will have expense ratios. Those fees will be deducted from the assets of your fund before robo advisors distribute the earnings to investors. If you are not sure that this is the method you wish to choose, some robo advisors offer a free trial period for you to check how they work before they start charging you.

You should keep in mind that most of the robo advisors you will find are using exchange-traded funds or mutual funds and not individual stocks to create your portfolio. They usually follow a passive investment method that is based on modern portfolio theory research. This method stresses the importance of the process of allocating to bonds or stocks.

Robo advisors will help you make a passive investment income through tools that will assist you in managing and building a diversified portfolio as well as show you how your accounts grow over the course of time. If you want to pay lower fees than the ones you would pay with financial advisors and have account minimus, this option is appropriate for you.

However, if you want to be a professional investor, robo advisors are not financial planners. They will not be able to offer you solutions tailored to your needs and direct you to particular investing strategies. Also, if you are close to your retirement, the allocation models of robo advisors may not assist you in the alignment of your investments with the phase of withdrawal. For this reason, they are recommended for investors who just start their careers and then, in later stages of their lives, seek a professional retirement income planner.

Passive Real Estate Investing

Real estate investing has been deemed as one of the greatest ways to create and accumulate wealth. As a matter of fact, real estate is one of the things most millionaires have in common since it is the primary way they became millionaires. In real estate investing there are active ways of investing such as managing an owning rental properties or renovating and flipping houses and there are passive ways to earn money that do not require from the investors to take on an active role.

When it comes to investing, passive refers to the fact that you will not play an active role in the business you will invest in. It does not mean that you will not have to do anything since it is not as simple as deciding to invest somewhere, invest your money, and never think of it again. For example, when you purchase shares of a company, you ill not have an active role in the daily operations of the company. You will only be able to financially benefit if the company succeeds. Another example of a passive investment is investing in your friend's company that you will not help him or her run.

Even though you will make passive investments, you are still required to research and learn both before and after you place your money in. When it comes to real estate investing, there are three basic ways to passively invest:

- ✓ Through real estate crowdfunding
- ✓ Through the stock market
- ✓ Forging a partnership with an active investor and own properties

A relatively new method in real estate investing is crowdfunding, which uses crowdfunding for raising capital targeted at real estate investments. By using this method of real estate investing, every investor will be able to invest in a wide range of properties without dealing with contractors, mortgage brokers, or real estate agents. All these will be the responsibilities of the crowdfunding platform which will take care of daily tasks to make sure the completion of the investment is successful and allow the investor to receive the returns with no need to go through the process of renovating and flipping homes on his or her own.

To better understand what crowdfunding is, think of it as a way for business owners to raise money without having to ask for just one investor to make a large investment, but through reaching out to a lot of investors who are willing to contribute a small amount of money. The way to reach out, multiple investors at one is done through an online platform.

There are crowdfunding websites and many business owners choose social media platforms for this job too such as Twitter and Facebook to advertise their project to a wider audience of investors who may be interested. If you invest in passive real estate keep in mind that it is a reliable method to generate money and there have been many cases of crowdfunded real estate investments that generated annual returns of approximately 15% and more for its investors.

If you are a beginner in real estate investing or an experienced investor, you need to understand or already know that securing the necessary funds to seal a deal can pose a real challenge to your plans. Due to this fact of the real estate market, many investors take advantage of the crowdfunding method as an alternative to secure funds for their deals. Several benefits of this method are the following:

- ✓ It will increase the options an investor has for funding his or her projects while growing his or her network of other investors.
- ✓ The investor with the deal and the one who will invest in it will indulge in direct marketing through this method which can also be used as a tool for the promotion of real estate businesses.
- ✓ With the completion of successful projects, the investor will gain a good reputation and the loyalty of his or her clients.
- ✓ From the online community, the real estate business will create; it will gain access to important feedback to address any potential flaws.

If you are on the other side of the spectrum, as a passive investor who helps in the funding of a real estate business project, aside from the immense returns you will get if the project is successful, you will be able to meet other investors whose ideas you would like to fund too and thus gain more passive income. Let us see the main two options of crowdfunding that will help you build your wealth passively.

The first option is equity investments and this is the most common method of crowdfunding investors choose due to the fact that it offers a higher return than the other option which is debt investing. However, the equity investment option is not without risks. This will give the investor an equity stake in a commercial or residential property, thus making him or her a shareholder.

The return of this investment will be calculated on the property's rental income minus the costs required for the crowdsourcing platform. If the property you invested in through this method is sold, you will get your share based on its appreciation value. Usually, the payments are done every quarter. Let us see the benefits of equity investments:

- ✓ There are no limits on returns: On a yearly basis, you may see returns at times up to 18 to 25 percent and possibly even more since this type of investment doesn't have a cap on them.
- ✓ Low fees: You will have the choice to pay one annual fee to keep your shares on the property you invested in, instead of fees paid from the start or monthly fees.
- ✓ Tax benefits: Due to the fact that you will own a share of the investment property, you will be able to

remove expenses on it from your annual income tax such as repairs or depreciation.

Some of the cons of equity investments include the fact that it is considered to be an investment with more risks since you will only be on the background when it comes to payments. In other words, if the investment property does not generate any profits, you will not get any returns on the money you invested. Also, if you wish to include more liquidity in your portfolio, then this method is not for you since it has a holding period of five to ten years.

The second method of crowdfunding investing is debt investments which mean that you as the investor will be the lender to the business that wants to carry out the project. You will receive a fixed return calculated by the interest rate of the mortgage loan the owner has and the amount of money you have put in. The payments in this method are completed every month or every quarter. Since you have indulged in debt investing when the payments are due you will be a top priority. Let us see some more benefits of this crowdfunding method.

✓ You will receive steady returns on your investment since it will be easier for you to predict when you will receive payments and how much you will earn due to the way the investment is structured. The potential annual return of this method is 8 to 12 percent.

✓ With debt investments, the risk is lower since the mortgage loan will be taken by the property owner and he is the one who has to secure it. If the owner is not able to pay off the mortgage, you will be able to recover any of your losses through foreclosure.

✓ This method also has a reduced holding time since debt investments are most commonly conducted with development projects. This means that the holding period will be from 6 to 24 months.

Some of the drawbacks of this method include the fact that they have higher fees when compared to the first crowdfunding method since the crowdfunding platform will probably take a particular percentage off of your payments. Also, debt investments are based on the interest rate of the mortgage loan the owner has secured. For this reason, your yields will have a cap.

Moving on, another way for you to earn passive income through real estate is to invest in such assets through the stock market. This can be done with buying into REIT or real estate investment trust. Through different ways, REITs work like mutual funds where investors purchase shares in a REIT and its managers invest the money in a portfolio that has to do with commercial properties. Generally, REITs manage or own commercial real estate properties that produce income whether this income comes from the properties themselves or from the mortgages on these properties. You will be able to invest in these companies personally with a mutual fund or through an exchange-traded fund.

Historically, real estate investment trusts have performed exceptionally well when compared to other asset classes. For example, between 1990 and 2010 the FTSE NAREIT Equity REIT Index, which is the index most investors use to calculate the state f the U.S real estate market, showed an average return of 9.9% annually and it was second only to mid-cap stocks. There are several types of REITs and if you can't decide which one is appropriate for you, you can enlist the help of a financial planner, a broker, or an investment advisor to analyze your financial goals and recommend which REIT is better based on your objectives.

One of the several types of REITs is Retail REITs. About 24% of this type of investment resides in freestanding retail and shopping malls, thus representing the biggest investment when it comes to types in America, at least. No matter which shopping mall you visit often, it is probably owned by a REIT. If you wish to start investing in retail real estate, you will have to first research well the state of the retail industry. For instance, is it a financially healthy sector now and what will be the outlook for the future?

In retail REITs, the investors make money through the rent they receive from the tenants. If the retails are in a tight spot due to poor sales and thus experience problems with their cash flow, they may delay or even default on their monthly payments. Eventually, they may even be forced to bankruptcy. If things get that messy, you will need to find a new tenant, which is not that easy, especially in this line of work. In order to mitigate this problem, you should invest in REITs with the most reliable tenants you will be able to find through your research.

Once your research on the industry itself is over, you have to focus your research on the REITs. As is the case with any other investment, it is very important that they generate healthy profits, have as little debt as possible, and strong balance sheets. Another thing you should keep in mind is that shopping has started to shift to online stores, not to the malls and this can potentially pose a problem for retail

REIT space. Even though owners of the REIT spaces keep up the good job of innovation by filling the properties with tenants that are not related to retail, still the sector is under pressure.

Another type of REIT is residential REITs. Those operate as well as own multi-family rental apartment buildings and manufactured housing. Before you make an investment in this type of REIT, there are several things you will have to consider such as the fact that we tend to find the most profitable apartment markets in locations where home affordability is relatively low when compared to other parts of the country. For example, locations such as New York have a high cost of single homes and thus people are forced to rent, which enables landlords to up the price they charge per month.

.Another thing you should research in this market is the job and population growth. Typically, people move to the city because it is easier for them to get a job and the economy in cities is flourishing. Generally, a falling in vacancy rate along with higher rents is an almost sure sign that the demand in a location is rising. When the apartment supply in a location is low and the demand is rising, residential REITs should be a success story.

The next type of REIT we are going to briefly analyze is healthcare REITs. As the costs of healthcare continue to rise, this type of REIT will also flourish. The purpose of such REITs is investing in the real estate of medical centers, retirement homes, hospitals, and nursing facilities. The success of healthcare REITs is inherently linked to the healthcare system. If the funding of health services is questionable, so will be the healthcare REITs. Generally, healthcare REITs will be successful in an economy where the demand for healthcare will increase such as the rise of the aging population.

Next, we will take a look at office REITs that invest in office buildings. Basically, they receive the rental income from tenants who most probably have signed a long-term lease. If you want to invest in this type of REIT you should research the state of the economy and more specifically the unemployment rate, the rate of vacancy, the economic condition of the location where the REIT has invested, and how much capital it has for acquisitions. You should find and invest in REITs that have placed their money in locations where the economy is booming and will continue to do so for the foreseeable future such as Washington D. C.

Mortgage REITs are the next type we are going to briefly check. About 10% of the REIT investments can be found in mortgages instead of real estate properties. Some of the most famous investments are Freddie Mac and Fannie Mae which are enterprises sponsored by the government and buy mortgages through the secondary market. However, keep in mind that the fact that they are most famous does not mean they are necessarily the best. This type of investment has risks of its own despite the fact that the investment is placed in mortgages instead of equity.

For instance, if interest rates are increased it would result in a decrease of the mortgage REIT book values and thus lessen the prices of the stock. Also, if such a case happens, obtaining financing in the future will be expensive. When the interest rates are low, but they have prospects of rising, most of the mortgage REITs will trade through a discount to net asset value per share.

While you choose any of the above methods of REIT investing to earn your passive income, you should keep in mind the following:

✓ They should have a total-return rate of investment. They will provide high dividend yields and moderate capital appreciation in the long term.

Search for companies that have been able to do both.

✓ Many REITs are traded most times on stock exchanges, in contrast with traditional real estate. You will get the diversification and benefits real estate investing has to offer without having to wait a long time since liquidity is important.

✓ Search for companies that have strong management to drive the business through difficult times. This means a management team with lots of experience.

✓ Invest only in REITs with reliable tenants and amazing properties.

Last, let us see how the value of REIT shares is most commonly assessed:

✓ Through the anticipated increased earnings per share

✓ Through the expected total return from a stock which is estimated from the anticipated change of price and the prevalent dividend yield.

✓ Through the existing dividend yields in relation to other investments that are oriented around yields.

✓ Through corporate structure and the quality of the management team

✓ Through the value of underlying assets of the real estate, other assets, and mortgages.

The last way you will be able to earn passive income through real estate investing is for you to become the partner of an active investor. Typically, investments in rental properties are an amazing way for you to build your wealth, but they can be very time-consuming. Even if you let a property manager do most of the work, you will still need to have an active role in the decisions that have to do with the maintenance of the property as well as do all the researching, analyzing, viewing, and purchasing your potential rental properties.

An alternative to the above situation is to partner with an investor that wants to play an active role throughout this process. All parties will win since it will allow you to invest your money in residential properties and let someone else, the active investor who has the extra cash, do all the work along with the managing partner. You could search online for active investors and make them an offer they can't refuse.

Generally, in passive real estate investing the main drawback is that you will get a lower return than you would if you were an active investor since the active ones will get a larger cut than you. For instance, if you are a passive partner in a real estate investment partnership, the managing partner will be paid more money than you for the time he has to put in. When you invest in a REIT, the management team that invests on your behalf will get a larger cut too.

However, this does not mean that the sacrifice of some return potential is not worth the relaxation of having someone else invest your money. This is especially true if the people, who play active roles, know how to turn your investment into a success story. Over the long run, passive real estate investing has the potential to help you build your wealth without having the usual problems a landlord or a manager of a construction project has.

High-yield Savings Account

It is a fact that high-yield savings accounts are able to offer higher interest rates than other accounts of this type and are easily accessed in the short term if you need funds. When it comes to saving and growing your money passively, you will have a number of options to choose from such as investing it, placing them into a high-yield savings account or in a checking account and it all depends on what your financial goals are. Every choice has its pros and cons.

For instance, as we have already seen when you passively invest your money, you may get better returns than with high-yield savings account, but you will not be able to access your money if they are not in liquid form, for example, if you have chosen to partner up with an active investor and decided to invest in rental properties. With a high-yield savings account, there may be restrictions when you have to withdraw your money such as penalties for withdrawing them earlier than a specif time or limits on the amount you are able to withdraw.

With investing, there is a higher risk involved, especially, in the short term. On the other hand, a checking account will allow you quick and easy access to your money, but the money you place in this type of account will typically not generate interest and if they do, it is often not much to be considered a way to generate and build your wealth in order to achieve financial freedom.

A savings account can be considered a smart decision when you want to achieve your short-term financial goals such as an emergency fund for a project you have in mind or when you want to go on a big trip. A savings account will offer you a separate account where you will be able to save money for your short-term goal and you ill not be tempted to use easily for everyday purchases as you would with your checking account. This account will also incur interest over time, so as for your deposit to grow beyond whatever you have saved.

However, the interest rates of a traditional savings account are very low. For instance, based on the information from the Federal Deposit Insurance Corporation (FDIC), in the United States, the average interest rate for such an account is 0.09%. In other words, if you made a deposit of $10.000 in a simple savings account and don't touch it for a year, you will see that after that year is over your money will be $10,009.

This may be better than no interest rate at all, but you may lose money as time passes. If you calculate the fees that were needed for your account as well as inflation, your deposit could lose its value over time with a low interest rate. The good news is that there is another option for you to achieve a higher interest rate and achieve passive income while still being able to access your money with ease. This solution is called a high-yield savings account. Let us see first what a high-yield savings account is.

This type of account is exactly what it says. It is typically a savings account that offers you a higher annual percentage yield or else APY than most traditional savings accounts. The risk involved is minimal since this stream of passive income is not an investment. Your earnings will be guaranteed by the APY proposed by the institution you collaborate with.

These accounts have minimal or no fees, at all, to open and maintain your account. The only thing you will have to do is make the deposits you wish and let your money grow as time passes. In the United States, high-yield savings accounts are also federally secured by the FDIC for

$250,000 per bank, if the bank you work with is a member of the FDIC, so you should do some research before devising with which bank you wish to collaborate.

When it comes to saving for your financial needs and goal as well as generating passive income, there are a lot of options to consider. The most important thing in such situations is to research which account type benefits you the most. Let us see the returns of a traditional savings account, a high-yield savings account, a one year certificate of deposit or else CD, and a checking account if we assume that you make a deposit of $5,000 and the typical APY in the United States on July 2019:

- ✓ High-yield savings account: 2.336% - $5,116.80
- ✓ Checking account: 0.00% - $5,000.00
- ✓ One year CD: 2.55% - $5,127.50
- ✓ Traditional savings account: 0.10% - $5,005.00

From the above example, you see that a CD with a duration of one year will offer you more interest than the one of a high-yield savings account. However, one of the disadvantages of a CD is liquidity something that is seen as an advantage of a high-yield savings account. As is the case with a checking account or a traditional savings account, a high-yield savings account will offer you the chance to use your money whenever the need arises and in many cases without any penalties.

With CD, you must wait for a certain period of time until your funds mature or else when your money is scheduled to be returned to you. On the other hand, with a high-yield savings account, you are able to save up for a few months or for more than a year, time isn't the issue. If you had managed to achieve your saving or passive income goals, you will not have to wait until your money is returned to you. However, a CD may be a better choice for you if you plan:

- ✓ On saving and generating passive income for many years
- ✓ On not withdrawing your deposit for the whole duration of the contract

Instead, if you need to save up money and generate your passive income goals in a short amount of time or you need quick access to your money, a high-yield savings account will offer you more flexibility and provide you with similar profits. We do not even have to consider for your given financial goals the other two options of a checking account and a traditional savings account since their interest rate is extremely low and in the case of traditional savings accounts nonexistent. The beauty of this passive income idea is that your money are simply sitting there, growing, and waiting for you to use them.

Typically, a high-yield savings account is ideal for your short-term financial goals and for the money you want to access quickly. Let us see some goals, a high-yield savings account could help you with:

- ✓ Generating passive income
- ✓ Creating an emergency fund
- ✓ Saving up for college
- ✓ Purchasing a car
- ✓ Saving up money for a wedding
- ✓ Planning your vacation
- ✓ Renovating your house
- ✓ Dealing with taxes
- ✓ Preparing to make a down payment for a house you want to buy

Essentially, any plans you have for making a big purchase for the next couple of months or within a couple of years, a high-yield savings account will do the job. Also, if you are unsure about this passive income idea, you could open this type of account and keep it running for a short period of time to both check and see if you need the accumulated money to use it on something else.

If you are planning for long-term goals to generate your passive income, you could open an investment account. However, you should keep in mind that investing, typically, has more risk involved than high-yield savings account even though the market returns are considerably more than the interest rate of a savings account.

If you have reached the decision of using high-yield savings accounts for your financial goals, there are a lot of things to think of such as the fact that there are many banks as well as credit unions out there that have a plan for a high-yield savings account. Let us see the various factors you can consider to make the best choice for your saving and passive income plan.

Checking the APY is the most obvious factor, but there are other things you have to consider before choosing a high-yield savings account that will affect:

- ✓ The pace through which you will achieve your goal
- ✓ The amount through which your balance will be able to grow
- ✓ The availability of your funds

What you would want to check is if the bank you are going to collaborate with has a minimum deposit requirement. There are various high-yield savings accounts that ask for a minimum deposit in order for you to be able to open your account. If you meet this requirement, then great! If you don't, you will have to pay the same amount of attention to the minimum deposit clause as to the APY when you will select your account.

Another requirement you may come across is the minimum balance one. Some accounts will ask of you to have a minimum balance to keep in order for you to maintain the APY they offer. If you fail to keep up with this balance, you may fall to a considerably lower APY. In this case, the best option for you to be safe and secure your passive income flow is to choose another bank with no minimum balance but a lower rate. The importance of this factor is enhanced if you plan on making frequent withdrawals since you are more at risk of falling below the requested balance.

In the United States, due to the Federal Reserve's "Regulation D," you should research the transfer and withdrawal limits before you sign to open a high-yield savings account. Also, you should be aware of the fact that banks are able to impose more limits and create their own rules as well as restrictions that govern those limits and this includes the potential penalties you may have to pay for if you pass them. Those limits should be taken seriously into consideration if you plan on withdrawing funds from this account often or transfer them to your checking account.

Also, there are many banks out there who will charge you several fees to open and maintain your account. Those fees may be charged monthly, quarterly, or annually and there are many cases when these fees could cancel or even surpass the gains you will have through interest. The fees could be added into your APY by some banks while others may add the fees later, which will reduce your yield significantly

Another thing to consider is that some banks will not allow you to simply open a high-yield savings account since they may ask you first to open a checking account. The checking account may come with a minimum balance and fees of its own. As a result, even if they have the greatest APY you will find, you will have to carefully consider whether this bank is worth the extras requested.

Withdrawal options are important when it comes to choosing the bank you will open your high-yield savings account at. You will have to research the different ways you are allowed to perform a withdrawal. For example, will you be able to make online transactions or you will have to go to the bank yourself? Do they have a mobile app you can use? Do they have an ATM close to you? You will want to access your money with convenience and not have to wait to get them in time.

The same applies to your deposit options. Some credit unions and banks make it convenient for customers to make their deposits. For instance, you will want to work with a bank that will transfer your check directly to your account or set up automatic deposits. This will help you make sure that you will put funds in your account each month and not be tempted to only deposit the monthly leftovers. The easier you are able to make deposits, the more you will be motivated to go through with your financial goals.

A high-yield savings account will be the perfect choice for you to achieve your passive income goals and at the same time save some money. It is perfect for short term goals, but this does not mean you are not able to use it for your long term financial goals too since it is considered to be one of the safest options to accumulate wealth with minimum risk. Open a high-yield savings account and let your money rest and multiply while you make no effort into making them.

Investing in Certificates of Deposit

Certificates of deposit or else CDs are considered to be investments that certainly help you to grow your money in a safe manner with little or no risk involved. If you decide on using them, the process can be very simple or extremely complicated. It all depends on your needs. For instance, if you have basic needs that have to do with a steady flow of passive income, you will find it easy placing your money into a certificate of deposit and begin the process of earning more passive money than you ever did with your savings account. However, if your financial goals involve a more complex and essentially an investing strategy the process will be more complex too.

When it comes to the basics of CDs, they are considered to be a type of account offered to you by a bank or a credit union. It is very similar to a savings account from the aspect that the money you deposit will earn interest. Typically, what makes certificate deposits different from a basic savings account is the fact that they pay more interest than any other of your bank accounts. However, there is a catch to this dream. You will not be able to touch your money for a specific period of time. For instance, if you agree on a one year CD, you will not have access to your money for six months.

The time range for this type of account will vary from six months to five years. Keep in mind that the longer a CD lasts, the more they will pay due to the fact that you make a greater commitment and on the other hand, the shorter a CD lasts, the amount it will pay will be less.

However, there are exceptions to this rule with some CDs offering the option to adjust the interest rate you gain as time passes. In case you choose to withdraw your money before a CD matures, you will have to pay a penalty. Think of CDs as a type of time deposit. You make a promise to keep your money in the bank for six months and up and the bank agrees to pay you through a higher interest rate because it knows it can use your money for long-term investments such as loans. You will not be asking for your money back in a week. The time period you agree to keep your money locked up is called "term".

CDs are considered to be safe investments; therefore, they are one of the best solutions you have if you do not want any risk involved when it comes to growing your money.

For instance, you may want to buy a new house in three years and you wish to save up money for the down payment through generating passive income. In such a case, you will not need to spend the money immediately as in three or four months.

So sealing your money in return for a higher interest rate is logical. If you have goals that take more than a few years, for example, retirement plans that are more than 20 years away, you should talk to a financial advisor to see if there is a better choice for this need and passive income. Keep in mind that your money is safe only if it is FDIC insured or if you are using a credit union, covered under NCUSIF insurance.

The Federal Deposit Insurance Corporation (FDIC) is an independent government agency with the task of overlooking consumer safety and banking. If your bank is insured by the Federal Deposit Insurance Corporation (FDIC), they protect you from losses if this bank closes, always assuming that your money is saved in qualifying accounts and are less than the protected dollar limit.

Even though your money is safe when closed in a bank, it still lends your money and invests it in order to earn a profit. However, if the investments do not work out, your money could be lost too. If your account is insured by the FDIC, you will be in a good place since it will replace your funds or send money to you. But the amount of money FDIC can cover has limits. You will be covered for up to $250.000 for each depositor for each bank and some types of accounts are not insured.

Due to the insurance of the FDIC, you will not have to run to the bank and save your money when the future of this bank turns bleak. Also, if you have funds that are not insured in the bank due to the fact that your deposit is more than $250.000 per individual depositor, you will be taking a risk. So, if you want to make sure that your funds are safe, research if your bank or the bank you want to collaborate with is FDIC insured. Another thing to keep in mind is that credit unions are not protected by the insurance of the FDIC. However, they get similar protection by the government under the National Credit Union Share Insurance Fund (NCUSIF).

The FDIC insurance will protect deposits at banks that are covered to the following accounts:

✓ Certificates of deposit (CDs)
✓ Checking accounts
✓ Money market accounts

- ✓ Savings accounts

The insurance of the FDIC will not cover:

- ✓ The money you have invested in bonds, Treasury securities, or stocks
- ✓ The contents of safety deposit boxes
- ✓ Insurance products like annuities
- ✓ The money you have invested in market mutual funds or exchange-traded funds

The items here are not insured because they are not considered as deposits even if you bought them through your bank. The insurance of the FDIC doesn't also cover theft such as identity theft, fraud, or bank robbery. However, some banks offer a banker's blanket bond that insures them from losses at ties of fire, robbery, embezzlement, or flood.

So, as far as FDIC insurance is concerned in order for you to be safe you should not have too many funds in one account or even one bank since you will be exposed to risk. Keep in mind that the limit of $250,000 is separate for every bank as long as it is under the FDIC insurance. For you to be under the FDIC coverage for more funds than the limit, you could use multiple banks or placing the money under another individual's name or spread your funds among other owners within one bank.

Returning to the topic of CDs, investing in them is quite simple since your first step is to let your bank know which one you want, for example, the six-month or the eighteen-month CD, as well as how much money you wish to deposit. We have mentioned before that some banks have minimum deposit numbers while other banks will let you put in your account as little money as you wish. When you have set up your CD, you will only have to wait until it matures and see your passive income grow. When the CD matures, you will get a notice that explains your various options. Some of them include:

- ✓ Renew the CD with another CD of the same duration
- ✓ Move your funds to a savings or checking account
- ✓ Purchase a different CD. For instance, move up for a six-month CD to a one-year CD
- ✓ Withdraw your funds

To decide which option is best for you, it would be better to review again the reasons why you are using this CD, your financial goals at the time, and reach a decision about what you should do with the money. It would be better not to let your CD renew automatically every time. You will have approximately ten days to decide what you should do. If the time passes and you do nothing, the CD will renew automatically continuing with the same terms you have agreed to before.

For example, if you had agreed to a one-year CD, asses your current situation. A lot of things can change in a year. Do you still wish to keep your money in a CD or you want to use your money somewhere else? Make conscious decisions and do not let the bank make the decisions for you. After a year or several ones, your financial goals may have changed and you'd like to make a riskier investment. If you need more time to evaluate your situation than a few days, you could move your money into a savings account and when you know what you want to do, you can invest them again in a CD.

Unless your bank is offering you something tempting to renew your original CD automatically, a pause will not damage your finances too much. Another thing you could look out for when your CD matures is what other banks have to offer after this time.

When you decided to work with your bank then, it may have had the best CD deal available, but other banks could be competitive now. Research how much passive money you can earn if you change banks and do so if the deal is really amazing. Changing banks can be a long process that takes energy and time, so your money will not generate any passive income through interest and this is the reason why changing banks should be the result of a great deal.

When it comes to CDs you could benefit from the option of "No Penalty" or liquid CDs. This is one of the various forms of CDs that banks and credit unions offer to customers and they keep creating new options to present to customers. As you have already realized throughout the course of this chapter, CDs typically have fixed rates and you would be charged with a penalty if you decided to withdraw your money earlier than the maturity term of the CD.

However, with liquid CDs, this is not the case anymore. This form of CD will allow you to withdraw your money any time you wish without having to pay an early withdrawal penalty. With this option, you will have the flexibility to withdraw and transfer your money to a CD that will pay higher if the opportunity arrives, but there is a price to pay for this flexibility.

Liquid CDs have a lower interest rate when compared to the CDs that place your money on lock up. If you look at this situation from the bank's point of view, it is logical because they are the ones that take the risk. This option would be best if you are almost certain that the rates will rise soon and you will be able to change banks or accounts in order to gain a higher rate.

Getting less passive income for this reason for a short period of time could be worth it. You should just make sure you understand the restrictions when you choose to make passive income through a liquid CD. For example, some banks impose restrictions on the time you will be able to withdraw your money and also on the amount you are able to pull out at any time.

Another form of CDs is the Bump-Up CDs which are similar to liquid CDs. After you purchase one, you will not be stuck with low interest rates if they rise in the foreseeable future. You will be able to maintain your original CD account and change to a higher interest rate when and if your bank offers them.

If this option seems appealing to you for your passive income plans, you should inform in advance your bank about wanting to exercise the bump-up CDs option. You will not get unlimited bump-up options and your bank will assume that you wish to remain with the initial interest rate if you do not inform it. As is the case with liquid CDs, bump-up CDs will pay lower interest rates when compared with the standard CDs. Again, this is a great option if rates will rise, however, if they stay the same or are about to fall, it would be better for you to choose the typical CD.

Step-up CDs will include scheduled increases in your interest rate so that you will not be restrained to rate that was in effect when you invested in your CD. Those increases may take place every six or nine months and in the case of long-term CDs, they will take effect once every year.

Another alternative you have is Brokered CDs. Those are sold for brokerage accounts and they can be bought through many banks. You can also keep them all in on account and not open one account to use the selection of a bank's CDs. Sometimes they will offer you better rates, but you should keep in mind that brokered CDs will have additional risks because instead of getting a CD directly from your credit union or bank, you get brokered CDs in a brokerage account.

As the name suggests this form of CDs is brokered. In other words, your financial advisor or yourself will assess the marketplace to discover the best CD rates. As is the case with other CDs, you will agree to lock your money up in that CD for a certain amount of time and the bank will agree to pay you a specific interest. Sometimes, you can invest in brokered CDs for a long time and they have maturity periods that are longer than the standard CDs coming straight from the bank. You could also trade brokered CDs through the secondary market, but the demand is very limited for you to attain a great price. You can also buy and sell them as is the case with other fixed-income investments. This option includes a limited supply and demand too.

However, you should watch out because this type of CD can be offered by any person who has the ability to purchase securities such as brokerage houses, financial consultants, financial advisors, or financial planners. Even you could do it through various online investing providers. One of the most important risks of brokered CDs is typically market risk and more specifically interest rate risk. For instance, you might risk selling your CD through the secondary market for less than you actually paid.

You could maintain your CD until it reaches maturity in order to avoid this risk. However, your plans may change and you wish to cash out and this is the stage where you will lose money. Brokered CDs work similarly to bonds. If the interest rates rise, secondary market buyers will not pay for face value when this investment is paying a low amount.

Another important risk you should keep in mind is fraud and scams. There have been many cases of individuals that have used brokered CDs as a way to steal money from the investors they worked with. Keep your ears open because if you hear something that is too good to be true, you are probably in danger of getting scammed. Also, brokers may not intend to scam you, but they may omit to tell you the full story of what you are getting into.

One more form of CDs is Jumbo CDs. Those, as the name suggests, have an extremely high minimum balance requirement that exceeds the amount of $100.000 in most cases. If you plan on gaining passive income through that amount of money, Jumbo CDs are the best option because you money will be safe and insured through the FDIC. Not to mention the significantly higher interest rate they will offer you.

All in all, there are several things you will need to consider if you decide to invest your money in CDs. For instance, CDs have lower risk and lower returns than other methods of investing your money and generating passive income. Your cash will be insured by the FDIC if you use a bank or covered by the NCUA insurance if you choose a credit union. Also, CDs have maturity requirements.

The CD will mature when its term is over and then, you will have to consider what you want to do next. Notify your bank for your decision before the renewal deadline or else your money will be invested in a new CD with the same terms you have agreed before.

However, it may have a higher interest rate than the initial one, but the time period you agreed at first. If the renewal deadline is not enough for you to decide, move your money to a savings account until you are ready. Another thing to keep in mind is that typically when you choose to invest in a long-term CD, the interest rate will be higher, but this option may not be the best one for your financial goals. For example, there could be high chances that you will need your money before the term is over, you will have to pay an early withdrawal penalty.

Also, there have been some rare cases of credit unions and banks that have refused to customers an early withdrawal request. If you decide to make a long-term commitment, you should also consider the state of interest rates. You will not be able to plan the time with perfection, no one can, but you could make some guesses on whether the interest rates will rise or fall. If you guess that interest rates are already high and in the foreseeable future are going to drop, a long-term commitment is perfect for you.

If you have money you don't need immediately and you wish to see growth through passive income, CDs are perfect for you. It would be good for your situation to consider a known CD strategy. If interest rates are low, there is no need for you to lock up your money in a CD that will pay you less for the next five years. What if CD and interest rates rise at some point? In this case, it would be better if you used CDs with short term commitment that will renew when the interest rates rise. The CD Ladder strategy will have you buying several CDs with each one having different terms, so they will reach maturity at different times. This will help you with having available money or money you can reinvest at dates when interest rates are up.

To better understand the ladder CD strategy, let us see an example. If you wish to make passive income out of $5,000, you can separate them in five different CDs of $1,000 each with different rates of maturity. When the one-year CD reaches maturity, you could place that money to a new three year CD, which will mature the year after another one of your CDs, matures.

You can keep this going for as long as you want until you need the cash which you will have since one CD will mature every year. With this ladder strategy, you will avoid locking all your money up and let them trapped in a low-paying CD while you will have a CD mature every year and thus avoid any early withdrawal penalties.

You can start using this passive income option with first contacting your bank or the credit union you want to work with and inform them that you want to place money into a CD. Banks will explain the different options you have and even allow you to make a CD investment online. If you don't like the online banking option, you could contact customer service or talk in person with a banker.

Explain to them how much money you wish to invest and learn everything on early withdrawal penalties and the different CD products they have to offer. When you move your money into a CD, you will see on your online dashboard or to your statements a separate account. CDs can be in nearly any account type such as individual retirement accounts, custodial accounts, and joint accounts. Just make sure to stick with NCUA-insured or FDIC-insured and do not forget to ask your banker for a better rate offer, especially if you have a heavy collaboration with them. Why not earn more passive income?

Earn Passive Income with Airbnb©

Another way for you to earn and build your passive income stream is by becoming a host on Airbnb©. Airbnb© has a one of kind approach when it comes to accommodation. As a part of the "sharing economy", it will offer to people in search of a place to stay someone else's home instead of a hotel. For instance, if a person wishes to find a place to crash while on his or her backpacking trip throughout Europe, Airbnb© gives that chance. It will also offer places for people who wish to stay in a house for even a month.

Airbnb© was founded by Brian Chesky, Nathan Blecharczyk, and Joe Gebbia in 2008. Now, recent estimates value this company of sharing homes around $35 billion. Before delving deeper into how you can make passive income as a host, let us take a brief look at how it works for guests. To start with Airbnb© does not own any properties. Instead, it works as a mediator between the people who wish to rent out their spare space and those who are searching for a place to rent.

To sign up on Airbnb© is completely free and simple. You will only have to give them your email address, your name, your birthday, and a password of your choice. You are also asked to agree to equal treatment of all people you encounter, regardless of sex, religion, and race among other factors. Once you have completed the above your account is ready and active.

Airbnb© has places you could choose to stay from all over the world considering that it has more than approximately 6 million listings through 190 countries scattered around the globe. Once you choose a listing, you can click on it and see a great amount of information about it such as pricing and check-in information, the amenities and size of that space, the rules of the house, availability, and a detailed description of that space.

You could also read reviews from others who stayed there as well as statements about the hosts. If you like this listing, you will be able to send a request to book it. Then, the site will encourage you to follow a few more steps such as giving more information about yourself. Once those steps are complete, you will be able to pay and complete your request for the space you wish to rent. After you are finished with your first booking, the process will take less time and will be much easier. However, your reservation will be final when it is approved by the host unless the space you chose is an "instant book" listing. Those listings do not have to be approved by the host.

When you wish to make passive income through this option, there are several things you will have to consider before you even list on Airbnb©. No matter what your motivation or your financial situation and goals are, you should really consider various things before you start. For instance, one of the most pressing matters to think about is your goals on listing your property or empty space on Airbnb©.

Even if you have generally thought about generating passive income through this, you have to ponder how serious you are about it. Are you looking to only make some passive money out by doing it only sometimes or you are serious about this choice and you want to make this option one of your main sources of income, if not your main one? Depending on your answers to the previous questions, you will have to assess the amount of capital you will need as well as the risk involved.

Also, you have to keep in mind that you will have strangers living in your home. Even though it is a great source of passive income that has the potential to earn you great money, if the idea of someone you don't know to stay in your house makes you uncomfortable, then you should probably not even try it. On the other hand, if you have no problem to host and communicate with strangers appealing, you should let this option on your list of ways to earn passive income and achieve financial freedom.

A large part of your success on Airbnb© will be based on rental arbitrage. This concept is when the potential of the revenues you will gain through something are considerably more than the cost you paid to get it, you have an opportunity presented. For example, let's assume that you have a well-maintained studio apartment in LA and its expenses are $1350 per month. It is located in an extremely nice neighborhood and has ideal amenities. At some point, you learn that your neighbor is listing her studio on Airbnb© for $150 per night. With some simple calculations, you see that if you could rent your place for approximately nine days per month, you will be able to pay your rent. Now, what if you could rent your space for 27 days per month? Well, you could gain about three times the fees for leasing your place per month. A great way to make passive income right?

Some other things to keep in mind have to do with hosting considerations since hosting on Airbnb© may include more commitment and many other people involved than you initially expected. Generally, there are three types of hosts on Airbnb©. The first one wants to rent out his or her available space from the current residence only when he or she does not use the property. Usually, this happens through a carefully planned time frame during which the unit is available for rent. For example, this person may be off for a few weeks for work and wish to rent his or her residence since all the hotels are booked and knows he or she could make a few extra bucks from it.

The second of the three types of hosts on Airbnb© is the person who seeks a stable income through this chance. He or she wants to achieve a recurring and consistent stream of extra passive income from his or her property by renting it out regularly. However, still not full time. For example, those people may want to rent out the property for two months each summer or for two weekends each month. If they get the opportunity to rent their property for a premium, they will take advantage of it as well. Their aim is to maximize their profit potential, even if it takes up more of their time to do so.

The third and last type of host will rent at least one property which is dedicated solely for a short full-time rental. The ultimate goal of this host is to have a steady rental income for the one or various units he or she has and let that be the main or primary stream of income. In the end, they wish to have an entire portfolio for these short term rent plan and develop ways to automate the process as much as possible. This type of host does not aim to expand the potential profit each of the units he or she owns has, but to maximize the profit they earn each hour they have to spend on organizing the hosting business they develop.

The truth of the matter is that the more income you wish to gain through this passive income option, the more capital, planning, work, and risk you will have to take on as well as develop different strategies to make your unit high in demand. When it comes to time, you need to keep in mind that you will not simply list your property and then you will see the money come in. You will have to dedicate some time to talk with potential guests who will ask you several questions about your unit before they book with you. Your time will also be required to gain amazing reviews because bad reviews will result in a decrease in your passive income.

Initially, this may be a problem for you but as you get the gist, you will be more efficient and find out ways to save you time that are appropriate for you without lowering the quality of service you provide. To have a successful Airbnb© listing, you will have to invest some commitment and time in the process such as making certain that everything is ready for your guests to arrive.

Another thing you should consider before you start hosting is how much your unit is worth renting. For example, you wouldn't leave your job for a new one without knowing how much you will be paid. Believe it or not, there are some listings that do not have enough demand to support a hosting business. On the other hand, there are units that are high in demand and could double your salary. Research and find out which category you fall in.

For instance, you could get a market report form a data provider you trust like the LearnAirbnb© recommended AirDNA. They have detailed data for many Airbnb© markets and they will be able to provide you with a realistic assessment on how much you will be able to make through Airbnb© hosting. Do not jump into Airbnb© hosting before you make sure that your unit will have enough demand to make everything worth it.

You may also consider the need to get insurance coverage, especially if it is your own home you are renting. Most probably the plan of your home insurance does not cover damages done from short term renting. It is a fact that Airbnb© liability insurance of $1 million gives you some comfort, but if you own some special to you items or if you consider the risk of not getting covered by this policy, you will have to get additional insurance.

Also, do not forget that you have neighbors to consider when you wish to make passive income with Airbnb©. If you reside in a quiet and gated community with neighbors that go to bed early and are extremely sensitive to outsiders or people that make noise, you have to consider how they will react to such a step you are going to take. This is also true when you are residing in a unit that is a part of a community with a shared space. Even if the house is your own, you have to consider the opinion of your neighbors because an angry neighbor could seriously damage your goals of hosting with Airbnb© and earning a considerable amount of passive income.

Added to the above, you should get the okay from your landlord before you start hosting. You may not be able to host in the apartment you currently reside in if your landlord does not allow it. You could approach him kindly and explain your reasons for this decision. However, if you have no luck with him or her, you could consider finding a new place that will allow you to host through Airbnb©.

In order to succeed in making a substantial amount of money with this passive income option, you will need to learn how to find the appropriate customers for your unit. in other words, you will need to find your target audience and as a result, you will be able to develop a profitable Airbnb© business. After you have selected your target audience, marketing will be very easy since you will know who you will have to turn your focus on and reduce vacancy rates.

People use Airbnb© for two reasons that are leisure or business and as is the case for every real estate investment Airbnb© is nearly all about location. Anyone who rents your place will do so because they wish to be close to something such as an attraction or an event. Research and discover everything that your neighborhood has to offer and this way you will have a general idea of who will choose to rent there. For example, you could answer the following questions:

- ✓ How many hotels are in the area? - If the answer is a lot, check and then compare your rates.
- ✓ Does your area have a mass or a broad appeal? - For instance, can people use it for different purposes both on weekends and on weekdays?
- ✓ Who resides in the area? - Do families, business owners or hipsters live there?
- ✓ Where is your unit located? - Is it on the main freeway or in a business district, etc.?
- ✓ What are the attractions in the area? - Do you see visitors coming for theme parks, business conferences or for its nightlife?

When you are looking for your target audience, you should also assess your property and think about which type of potential renters it can attract. For example:

- ✓ What are the amenities you will offer? - A pool, lots of space, or covered parking?
- ✓ What type is your property? - Is it a private room, a couch, or a full unit?
- ✓ What is the state of your unit? - Is your place the nicest one in your neighborhood or simply passable?

It is a fact that a certain amount of amenities will attract more people to your unit since more and more hosts bring units to the market and guests have many options to choose from. If you are serious about this option, your furniture, as well as amenities, could make all the difference in the world when it comes to hosting through Airbnb© since you will deliver to your guests an amazing experience and earn 5-star reviews. There are various ways for you to make your guest be as comfortable as possible to earn amazing ratings and some are way easier than others. The right items for your listing will be able to make the difference between a one star rating and an amazing 5 star one.

Aside from the obvious items, you will have to stock, we will present you with a list of the various other possible items that many hosts have a tendency to forget. You may wonder if you need all these things to provide your guests with an amazing experience, but the truth of the matter is that your guests may not notice that you have them, until they will certainly need them. If they find them already equipped to your unit, they will immensely appreciate the gesture and this is the attitude that wins great reviews.

The first category of essential items you must have for Airbnb© hosting is safety items. Many of the things you will see listed below are essentials that we must have in our homes too. If you see something missing for the list, you have to acquire immediately because you will be placing your guests and your Airbnb© business at risk. Let us see the safety items to acquire:

- ✓ Simple Carbon Monoxide Detector
- ✓ Nest Protect Smoke and Carbon Monoxide Alarm
- ✓ Simple Smoke Alarm
- ✓ At least one Fire Extinguisher
- ✓ First Aid Kit
- ✓ First Alert Standard Fire Extinguisher
- ✓ 299 Piece First Aid Kit
- ✓ Kidde 4LB Fire Extinguisher
- ✓ Non-Slip Bathtub Mat to Keep from Falls
- ✓ Fire Escape
- ✓ Non-Slip Clear Bath Mat
- ✓ Kidde 3 Story Fire Escape

Also, another essential service you want to include subscription and the chance for your guests to catch up on your Amazon Prime or Netflix shows. You should not restrict your guests to watch the local news on TV if their plans change and have to spend more time inside your house. Let us see the different items you can get to offer your guests easy access to such channels:

4K TVs:

- ✓ New Amazon 4K Fire TV
- ✓ New 4K Roku
- ✓ Non 4K TVs:
- ✓ New Roku Express
- ✓ New Amazon TV Stick w/ Alexa Voice Remote

If you choose to offer through your listing an effective escape from the modern world, every guest that will choose your unit to stay at will expect to have a working HDTV in your listing. There is no need for you to spend a fortune and get a fancy TV, you only want one that works, is high definition, and has access to Netflix. It is also recommended that you have one TV in the bedroom and one TV in the living room. Let us see a list of some affordable TVs for your listing that meet all the above requirements:

- ✓ Sceptre Ultra Slim 32″ inch HDTV
- ✓ 2018 TCL 40S305 40″ Roku Smart LED TV
- ✓ Toshiba 32″ Smart LED TV – with Fire TV
- ✓ TCL 32″ 1080P Smart LED TV with Roku

- ✓ Sceptre 55″ 4K LED TV icon
- ✓ TCL 55″ 4K Ultra HD Roku Smart LED TV icon
- ✓ Toshiba 55″ 4K LED TV

Another thing you should consider unless your aim is still to offer an escape from technology is the appropriate WIFI router. Your guests will most probably wish to use your WIFI, but what will be the point of you having high-speed internet if your router is not able to support it? You will need a router that can support the use of multiple devices and intense views for video content. If you need to buy a new router, you must choose one that is right for the size of your property. Let us see some routers that will work, depending on the size of your unit:

For one-bedroom and studio listings:

- ✓ TP-Link AC1200
- ✓ Tenda AC1200 Dual Band Wi-Fi Router
- ✓ For two to three-bedroom listings:
- ✓ Linksys AC1900 Dual Band
- ✓ Linksys AC1750 Dual Band
- ✓ For larger and four-bedroom listings:
- ✓ Linksys Max-Stream Tri-Band
- ✓ Linksys WRT AC3200 Smart Wireless Router

You will also have to offer your guests the ability to get some coffee even if you are not a coffee drinker. To some, good coffee can be a great way for them to start their day the right way, especially for a tired travel guest. You don't need an expensive espresso machine to achieve that. A simple coffee maker will satisfy your guests along with a french press.

There is downside to have these simple amenities to offer to your guests since those who want to drink coffee will appreciate the quality items you are offering and those who don't want one will simply not use them. You could also go a step further and offer them whole roasted coffee beans with the appropriate airtight container used for storing.

Some other items you would want to offer to your guests are digital clock and phone charging cables. Aside from the bed essentials you have to offer in order for your guests to have an amazing sleep experience, there are two other items your guests will appreciate immensely, a digital alarm clock and some extra phone charger cables. There are high chances of your guests forgetting their phone charges and this is something that happens all the time, even to people who have the best memory there is. In this case, too, you will not have to buy overpriced charging cables. You could even order them online. Last but not least, let us see a list of the most commonly forgotten items hosts forget to add to their property. Keep in mind that the items listed below are not optional. Here they are:

- ✓ An Iron
- ✓ A Dryer
- ✓ A Curler
- ✓ A Straightener
- ✓ Wi-Fi Enabled Printer

In order for you to better understand what your guests need, you could place yourself in their shoes and imagine what it would be like if you traveled in a new town or country and you have just checked-in to your Airbnb© listing. What would you like to find there for the rest of your stay?

Now let us see the process you have to go through if you want to follow this great passive income option and rent out your unit to Airbnb©. The first thing you have to do is create a free Airbnb© account. When you do that, you will see in the upper right corner the words "become a host" and click on it. After that, you have to create a listing for your unit which will seem to you a lot similar to a profile page of your space. Keep in mind that the nicer your profile is the more attention it will get, just as social media profiles. For this reason, you will have to come up with:

- ✓ A great title
- ✓ A great description
- ✓ Great photos of your unit
- ✓ A great host profile

One thing you should focus on is house rules. You should set simple and clear house rules because your guests need to know what is off-limits. However, you should not make obnoxious rules that will make no one book your unit. Also, you may have those rules on your listing, but you should also place them in the house. Most people may not even remember the rules or read again your listing before they check-in, so you have to make sure they are on the right track. Let us take a look at a few rule categories that will help you in the process of setting them:

- ✓ Extra guests: Are they allowed? How many? Do they need to be approved?
- ✓ Smocking: Is it permitted? If so, where?
- ✓ Areas that are off-limits: Are there areas, guests are not allowed? What will be the penalty for going?
- ✓ Areas to eat: Are guests allowed to eat in all areas? Is there a spot just for eating?

- ✓ Cleaning Directions: Should the guests clean the dishes? Where should the trash go?
- ✓ Laundry: Where should they put it?
- ✓ Parties or gatherings: Are they allowed? Do they need approval? What is the max size?
- ✓ Animals and other pets: Are they allowed? Are there extra charges? What size?

When you reach the part of having to price your unit, Airbnb© will help you set up your pricing by presenting you with the average prices in your area. On Airbnb©, you could also make passive income through hosting an experience. According to the Airbnb© site: "Airbnb© Experiences are activities designed and led by inspiring locals. They go beyond typical tours or classes by immersing guests in a host's unique world." If you wish to do that, review the quality standards of Airbnb© that present you with all the requirements for experiences.

The charges Airbnb© has are considered hefty, but probably cheaper when compared to a hotel stay. Guests will have to pay in addition to the rent money, a service fee of approximately 13%. Hosts will also have to pay a service fee of about three percent, which Airbnb© gets after every transaction. If you choose to be a host who offers experiences, you will have to pay a 20% service fee. Guests and hosts will not trade money up close. Guests will complete payments on the Airbnb© site when the reservation is done and they even have the option to split costs with others. Then, the host will receive the payment from Airbnb©.

This is another amazing option for your passive income plans to achieve financial freedom. It is also a choice that can help you build your own business and if you want to take things a bit further, it could "train" you for rental real estate investing if you take this option seriously and plan your steps well.

Index Funds Investing

Throughout the investing world, index funds have transformed into a major force. According to many billionaires, index funds present the most appropriate way to invest in stocks. As David Swenson said: "When you look at the results on an after-fee, after-tax basis, over reasonably long periods of time, there's almost no chance that you end up beating the index fund." Also based on Warren Buffet's words: "Both large and small investors should stick with low-cost index funds." But what are index funds?

An index fund is considered to be a form of a mutual fund, which in turn is a collection of investments such as real estate, bonds, stocks, etc., that you are able to buy. It is a package deal. Also, an index fund is able to track an index, which represents a part of a market, for example, the bond market, the stock market, the real estate market, etc.

A famous index, perhaps the most famous one, is the Dow Jones Industrial Average, which is a list of thirty blue-chip stocks. This list was created to represent a number of stocks that are of importance for the economy of the United States. The S&P 500 is perhaps one of the most discussed index around the world. It is short for the Standard and Poor's 500. This index is more complex in it methodology than the one of Dow Jones.

To put it simply, an index fund is essentially a mutual fund that does not use a portfolio manager to make the selections. Instead, this job is done by an individual committee that determines the methodology of the index. This is the case if you purchase a Dow Jones Industrial Average index fund or ETF, which is a mutual fund that is traded like a share of stock through the day and it is not settled when the day ends as it happens with common mutual funds. This is the reason why an index fund is considered to be a passive source of income because you are handing the job of the management of your money to a group that create an index and more specifically to the editors of The Wall Street Journal.

If you decide to purchase an S&P 500 index fund, which has in its collection the 500 largest companies in the United States, your money will be managed by a group of individuals at Standard and Poor's. However, you will still own your portfolio of individual stocks. Index funds have many advantages, especially for beginner investors who don't have much money to set off their career immediately and for those who wish to have an amazing source of passive income. Let us briefly see some of those advantages:

- ✓ They have the lowest costs
- ✓ They have maximum returns
- ✓ They require no effort
- ✓ They have minimum taxes

Sounds too good to be true? It is indeed true. The fund managers will invest in securities as they are in the market. It is a fact that index funds are passive since the managers of the fund do not buy and sell stocks in order to beat the market. They have as a goal to be the market. Given the nature of an index fund that has many investments included, if some stocks in the index do not perform well, your portfolio will be protected by the others. The reality is that by buying one index fund, you will be able to invest in the biggest companies in the United States.

Index funds require little cost because you will not have to pay for admin costs and the fee for your portfolio management. For example, a small investor who wants to buy shares of the 500 biggest companies in the United

States and thus will have to buy 500 stocks, he or she will have to spend an extremely large amount of dollars for commissions and invest millions to achieve this. This is solved with index funds. Once you find the right index fund for your risk tolerance and needs, you will not have to spend your time on decisions and tasks that most investors have to deal with daily.

The most common categories you can buy index funds are:

- ✓ United States Stocks
- ✓ United States Bonds
- ✓ Real Estate Investment Trusts
- ✓ International Bonds and Stocks

Bonds are the way of the corporations or the government to say "I owe you". Most bonds are low at risk and for this reason, they have low returns. However, this is what places your portfolio at less risk. Real estate investment trusts are the index funds for the real estate market.

Money from investors is gathered and later used to invest in real estate properties that produce income such as international or domestic industries, commercial properties, and housing. International bonds and stocks will be perfect if you wish to diversify your portfolio. However, international stocks do not relate, typically, with how United States stocks perform. If you invest in both international and United States stocks you will be able to smooth things down.

There are some things you should keep in mind if you decide to invest in Index Funds as a way to achieve your passive income goals such as costs. Typically, index funds are considered to be low-cost investments, under 0.20%. However, you may come across some expensive ones that will cost you around 1.5%. In such a case, you should not even consider buying one that has that many costs. You should obviously invest in an index fund that costs 0.20%.

Another thing to consider the tracking capabilities since it is the job of an index fund portfolio to imitate accurately an index. To make sure the necessary accuracy is provided, you could compare the returns and holdings of the index to your fund, especially if you are investing in a small broker. Also, please, do not check you investments each day that passes.

You have used this as a source of passive income and you are better off watching a movie. No one has benefited from checking his or her investments every day. You should do that once every two or three months since index funds are the lowest risk way to invest in stocks. Take advantage of this opportunity and do not stress out over it. Last but not least, consistency is important in this case and you should set an automatic investment for every month into your index fund. This way you will be able to make more returns when it comes to your passive income. You will be given the chance to make money from the comfort of your own home without the many costs associated with other forms of investment. This is why index funds are considered one of the most effective ways a person could earn effectively passive income.

Epilogue

As you have seen throughout the course of this book, earning passive income is not as difficult as many people think and there are various ways available to make this happen and lead you to your goal of being independent and use your times as you wish. The truth of the matter is that no form and source of income is free of risk and does not require a certain amount of effort and time. Passive income is able to provide you with money you have not spend an entire day to make and have someone else take advantage of all your hard work. You will be able to see the benefits of any effort you have placed into creating a passive income stream.

When you are able to create and earn passive income, you can earn it at any given time during the day or night and from any place around the world. You will not have to be stuck on a specific schedule or job in order to make money. Once you have successfully developed one or even many different passive income streams, you will be able to see the money flowing into your account. Imagine the feeling you will get once that happens! this is the true meaning of financial freedom and you will be more close this goal than you even realize.

Whenever passive income is concerned, you will have no limit to it. There is nothing that prevents you from creating as many passive income streams as you want. The time you dedicate for such streams to be created is entirely up to you. Also, the way you want to create your passive income is entirely up to you too.

There is no limit not only to the hours you will place but to the ideas you will follow too. Passive income can be achieved through many different sources. Choose the options that make more sense for you and are based on the things you like doing the most.

You don't have to follow the schedules and ideas you dislike and do not inspire you or motivate you to achieve financial freedom. You will be able to become your own boss. Through making money from your passive income streams, you will not have to answer to anyone else other than yourself. No one will be able to question your decisions or the way you work because you will have no boss. Everything will go through you and the responsibility for the successes as well as failures will be yours.

However, you should keep in mind that creating the various passive income streams you wish will take effort and time to complete. Many people think that streams of passive income are easy to set up and need little work to start making money. This belief is a very simplistic view and can mislead many into thinking they can make money overnight. You will be required to contribute a considerable amount of your time and you may have to invest some money into your ideas too. By dedicating your time and in some cases your money, you will make sure that your passive income sources will be flowing effectively.

Even if you put all the effort you are able to, you should now that it may take a while before the passive income of your choice start to make money and becomes a stream. You need to be prepared from the beginning that it may be a while before you succeed in making this your main source of income and be able to quit your job and achieve your goal of financial freedom. In order for you to e able to quit your job and make this your main source of income, you have to diversify your tries and be certain that money will come in your account at all times.

This is a true fact because only one source of passive income will not be enough to be financially secure and free. The risk involved in having only one stream of passive income is that it can eventually dry up and leave you with no job and no income at all. So, in the case of creating many sources of passive income, you will rest assured that even if one dries up, you will have the others to cover the losses until you manage to develop it again.

Another thing you should keep in mind when you decide to create and earn passive income is that it can isolate you. This is true in most cases due to the nature of passive income. When you gave a 9-5 job, you will be able to meet new people and socialize, no matter how much you hate your boss or your job in general. You went out and met new people. While it may be a dream come true to be able to work from home and get your various chores or tasks completed through the comfort of your living room, you will have to spend a lot of your time at home, especially at the initial stage of creating your various passive income streams. For some people, who can't stand not seeing people for long periods of time, this situation may drive them crazy. If this is the case, then creating a stream of passive income, is not recommended for you.

Before you make the decision to go down this road there are several things to consider since you will have to take a step back, relax, and think about your goals. You have to be completely honest with yourself on the various things you expect to gain through this method. For instance, o you only wish to add a couple of hundred dollars to your existing income or do you wish to reach a place where you will be able to quit your job and achieve financial freedom. How long to do you plan on building your passive income streams and be able to quit your job? Where do you see yourself ten years from now?

Do you want to build multiple passive income streams because it sounds like obtaining easy money and you expect them to simply fall into your lap or those streams sound like the perfect fit for the goals you have set in your life and your general lifestyle? If you are serious about earning passive income to achieve your financial goals, the first thing you should expect is for you o have in the beginning a learning curve and a strong battle to achieve self-discipline. You will find many distractions through the internet as well as lots of sources of information. However, you should stick to your plan and choose only the sources that are completely relevant to your ideas of passive income streams.

In order to be successful in creating your passive income streams and attain financial freedom you will certainly need the following:

- ✓ A mentor
- ✓ A clear vison based on research
- ✓ A business plan
- ✓ A market
- ✓ A general plan
- ✓ A separate bank account for your passive income streams
- ✓ Determination
- ✓ Commitment
- ✓ Integrity
- ✓ Patience
- ✓ Self-discipline

In any new start you decide to make throughout your life you will need a solid plan and a lot of work to make this new start a success. Stay motivated by thinking the end result of developing and maintaining various passive income streams. Financial freedom is the end goal and you should do everything you can to acquire it. Passive income streams will offer you your dreams.

Personal Notes

PART 2:

Real Estate Investing

The Blueprint to Starting a Passive Income Business and Making Money Through Rental Optimization and Property Management

Timothy Turner

Table of Contents

Introduction

Through business papers, radio, and television, we constantly see news or analysis that has to do with real estate. You may be wondering why this is happening and how can real estate be such a blooming and sure business despite the global economic crisis. The truth is that real estate is a sure investment despite the occasional downs it suffers. For instance, house flipping which is the practice of buying real estate, improving it, and selling it again for a higher price, has been very popular throughout the past ten years as an investment; however, it has been around for more than that.

Would you believe me if I told you, the practice of real estate investment dates back to the Revolutionary War? Even before that, we could imagine that cave drawings were a form of real estate investing. Even though Homo erectus did not rent out caves to other tribes, historians do maintain that a currency exchange of shorts existed among the early humans for them to gain shelter. In various agrarian systems, fertile lands were marked by settlers and those who were able to defend the land were able to keep it.

As time passed the system of tribal leaders was developed and those who were appointed by the tribe could disperse lands, ask for payments, and settle disputes. When stronger tribal leaders emerged, strongholds were created as well as temples, irrigation channels and farming methods were improved. This actually meant that farmers were then able to support more children and thus the increase in fertility meant greater numbers of workers. On the other hand, families that were focused on hunting were able to support two children at best. The people who were hunters followed a tribal system too but suffered because of uncertainty in life and scarcity. That was translated to them being able to support only two or three at most extended families.

Farmers soon realized that they could not protect their tribe's territory effectively from raiders. For this reason, they sacrificed their tribe's community to gain the safety of numbers. They joined the protection of an army controlled by a king and all paid homage to him who claimed the ownership of the land. This was the first system of rent, in its most basic form. Those villages of farmers turned to cities with the original leading families kept their ownership due to their right of lineage since their ancestors were the ones who protected the tribe from raiders.

The system that was then developed, labor in exchange for protection, was separated into two different systems in the majority of countries and included tenancy and taxes. The royal family gave to those who were loyal to them, wealth, titles, and deeds to lands. Those deeds allowed those who had them to collect money from the subjects that lived there, essentially they collected rent. Aside from this rent, everyone that lived within the borders of a ruler's territory had to pay taxes.

Various other demands were made by rulers such as military service and the people could rarely do something because those who governed did so not only by birthright but also because of their strong military. Even though rulers could be overthrown by other kings and sometimes by the people, another would take the throne and the average people most times would not notice anything different.

However, things were not that bleak since they were able to indulge in trading with other kingdoms. As the level of wealth increased for the people too, a class of merchants was created that included specialized tradesmen and laborers who could make ends meet not through farming but through skill. As a result, shops, as well as houses, emerged that had nothing to do with farming that still paid the required taxes and rent to the landlords and kings, however, they were rented, bought, and sold among commoners and not only by those who belonged to royalty. Rich merchants were the first landlords who were not royalty but commoners, thus gaining status and wealth among others. Even though those merchants did not own the land, they owned the houses included in these lands.

As time passed and aristocracies were replaced by accepted meritocracies, systems through which the smartest and best ruled a nation for the good of the people, politics as we know them today began to form. The titles of the lands were divided into smaller parts and were sold on something similar to a free market. However, the people who had the money to buy the deeds were former aristocrats or merchants who had managed to survive throughout the revolution. The class of peasants was still not able to escape from the farming life created thousands of years before.

The industrial revolution served as a curving point for the class of farmers and is viewed by many experts as one of the great equalizers in our history that can be matched only by the creation of firearms. Even though the effect of this industrial revolution can be seen as neither negative nor positive, they can be viewed as either depending on the application.

For instance, the application of machines to aid manual labor set many peasants free of various tasks and allowed those few who were the privileged ones time for specialization and education into different fields of labor paved by the introduction of machines to the industry. However, cabinetmakers, seamstresses, and cobblers saw their once valuable at skills to be rendered obsolete and for this reason, they had to return to farming or to the coal mines in order to make a living.

Those from the lower classes that managed to climb to the upper classes were sensible enough to the low-classes and lead them a hand into finding housing for laborers as well as products that were aimed at them. The classes at the time were blue collar, middle class, and white collar as well as some others. The higher classes owned cars, houses, and later radios and televisions.

Mortgages are not the invention of a particular country. They existed long enough as a loan provided only to those of noble ancestry. After the industrial revolution took place, banks were open to providing mortgage loans of a higher risk to common people due to the increase of wealth over the world. This situation helped the people to have their own homes and if they wanted they could become landlords. Despite the fact that it took thousands of years for people to own their home, it was then opened to many. It has even reached a point where people were able to buy too many properties. However, the problem with mortgages is that accumulating too much debt could make someone lose a house the same way it would help him or her own one.

After this brief history of real estate investing, the bottom line is that land ownership was the factor that helped us have all the investment opportunities we can see today. Land ownership has changed from being earned by strength to something you are able to buy, trade, sell, as well as rent. There always has been a situation where a fee was paid to the owner of land for its exploitation and protection. This tenancy was first offered to tribal leaders, then it was paid to kings, and at the end to landlords.

In the first chapter of this book, we will analyze the different types of real estate investments to help you understand the basics of this business as well as the pros and cons of investing in each one. In the second chapter, we will present you with some key rules of real estate investing as well as the different strategies you can follow in order for you to achieve the goals you have set when you decided to follow this path. In the third chapter, we will analyze the various and most important risks involved when you decide to invest in real estate. This way you will be able to prepare better to avoid or handle the consequences of those risks. In the fourth chapter, we will present how you will be able to start a real estate business and become a successful real estate investor from scratch. Many are afraid to make the leap and make the important decision of investing in real estate. Is it, however, as difficult as everyone thinks?

Real estate investing is an amazing journey filled with challenges and immense profits you should never give up once you start. Let us see the different reasons why this is true throughout the course of this book.

The Different Types of Real Estate Investments

As we have already established, real estate investing has to do with buying, owning, managing, renting or selling land as well as any structure on it for profit. For many people, investing in real estate has been deemed as uncharted territory. Investing in bonds and stocks, commonly called traditional assets, real estate investments are believed to be an alternative asset that is difficult to afford and access.

Even though this may be true, there is no reason to avoid investing in real estate just because you are not familiar with the way it works as an investment opportunity. When you have a solid investment plan, real estate can be profitable as well as a dependable way for you to multiply your money both in the short and the long term. When done correctly, real estate investing will be able to provide you with a consistent income stream, portfolio diversification, and appreciation potential. However, when someone does not know where to start, real estate investing can seem like a herculean task.

To start with, there are four categories of real estate you can invest in. Those are the following:

- ✓ Residential Real Estate
- ✓ Commercial Real Estate
- ✓ Industrial Real Estate
- ✓ Land

When it comes to residential real estate we usually include single-family homes, condominiums, townhouses, and multi-family homes. There are different types of regulations and laws that define residential real estate when compared to commercial real estate. In real estate, residential property refers to structures that have been zoned or developed for living as the examples we provided previously with the addition of mobile home parks and apartments. Any property that is properly constructed for occupation and for a non-business purpose can be deemed as residential property. In this chapter, we will focus on residential real estate due to the fact that it is the most common investing option for people who want to make their first steps in real estate investing. Below is a list with the structures included in this type of real estate:

- ✓ **Condominiums**: They are privately owned units included within larger communities or buildings.

They are similar in structure to this of the apartment buildings. When a person buys a condo, he or she owns the individual unit and all the other unit owners will share joint ownership of all the common areas which are controlled by the management.

- ✓ **Townhomes**: Those are units that are often larger than condos and still have walls with the other buildings.
- ✓ **Cooperatives**: They are units included in one building where the people who live in the building own the structure together.
- ✓ **Single-family houses**: They are commonly constructed on a single lot and do not share space with others living in the area.
- ✓ **Multi-family houses**: Their size often varies from two to four units. For example, you can imagine a duplex or a four-plex. However, anything that is bigger than four units is commercial property.

Apartments are considered as residential property only if they less than five units. Also, camps, hotels, and other places that are used only temporarily by people are not considered residential property. Those types are more efficiently categorized as commercial real estate.

Condominiums

When you use condos as an investment property, you could opt for renting it out to tenants. This way, condos will work as an apartment does. The difference here is that a person can own a different condo, but apartments are rented by someone who claims ownership of the whole building. If you want to buy a condo, you will have to pay a monthly condo fee along with the money you paid to purchase the condo. This monthly fee will cover the upkeep and maintenance of the areas that are shared with the various other owners in the condo community.

So, should you purchase a condo as a way of investing in real estate? Let us see the positive aspects of investing in condos. One of the most important benefits of owning a condo is that others will have to deal with the maintenance of the property's exterior and not you or the tenant thus you will have fewer worries about its maintenance. Neither you nor the tenant will be responsible to mow the lawn or shovel the snow for example. Another benefit of owning a condo is that you will not have to worry about including in your budget expenses such as replacing a roof which can cost a great amount of money. This is the case because you will own only the space that is inside the condo and not the exterior of the structure. The only thing you will have to worry about is the maintenance of the systems and appliances within the unit you own.

Usually, the condo association is responsible for taking care of the troubles and expenses that have to do with the maintenance of the building as well as the grounds. However, each condo association decides which are theirs and the owner's responsibilities. So you will have to read carefully every document the condo association offers you before you make any purchase.

Typically, it is less expensive to buy a condo than for instance a townhouse or a single-family home that has similar features, as an investment. As a result, you will be required to pay less pocket cash. You should make sure that the monthly rent you are charging is able to cover any ownership costs you have such as the fee you have to pay every month for the condo. The purchase of a combo may seem cheaper than that of other real estate investments because there are recurring fees.

Another benefit of investing in condos is the inclusion of high-quality community conveniences such as a club room, fitness room, and a pool. Those amenities can attract many tenants and thus you will be able to keep the unit you own rented with no delays that could cost you money. Keep in mind that properties who include such alluring amenities will usually be high in demand. In other words, if a tenant moves out of your unit, you will be able to have very short vacancies and those are an investor's dream when it comes to maintaining the cash flow.

One more thing that makes condos a reliable real estate investment is the increased security of most condo buildings. Most commonly, you will need a key to enter the building before you are able to get at the front door of your unit. Then, each of the units is equipped with intercom which residents can use and allow in visitors or guests they approve of. This extra security will make any tenant feel very safe, something they will wish to pay for generously in order to enjoy.

Also, there are more rules you will need to abide by when you own a unit in a condo community. For instance, you will need the permission of the condo association to make any alterations to your unit whether it is inside or outside of it. Most probably you will not be able to make any changes to the color of your front door and residents are usually forbidden to keep a home office and conduct businesses. It is a fact that the rules of a condo community are more strict than other similar properties which are not called a condo, however, these rules offer the necessary protection for the units to not be depreciated by preventing unwelcome activities.

The regulations and rules of a condo association are often proven to be exactly what is needed for the existence of a community that will benefit all owners. For example, your tenant will not be able to grow anything he or she likes on the patio, but he will not have to worry about his neighbor's garden turning into a junkyard. You can think of the condo association as a police force that keeps residents from bad behaviors, neglecting and damaging the property and thus maintain the value of the unit.

Moving on to the cons of investing in a condo, the first one is very common for many people. Neighbors, whose behavior is not ideal. Admittedly, you will have neighbors in any community you decide to live in whether they are beside you, above you, or below you. In all the time you will own a condo, there are high chances that your tenant will have a neighbor you wished had never moved in.

This poses a problem because when your neighbors are not welcomed, you will have a hard time to keep your tenant happy. When your tenant is not happy, this may result in higher vacancies than you'd like and a constant search for tenants. Also, since you are the owner, you will have to handle personally on various times any complaints with those neighbors, something that can be very frustrating.

Another drawback of investing in condos is the fact that condo fees will most probably be raised every few years due to inflation. Added to the monthly fees, you may also get a pretty expensive "special assessment." This assessment is an added fee given to each owner for special projects, such as paving all over again the parking lot. If you have not taken any budget measures for such fees, you could end up in a position where you will no longer be able to afford the special assessments or condo fees.

There is also the danger of financial mismanagement by the condo association to think of. The association board that rules the condos often includes condo owners of the community who are elected or volunteer for the position. Usually, the condo buildings are owned by a group of investors who hire a property management company to take care of the collection of the condo fees as well as take care of the management of the community. The governments of each state request from the condos to create and follow legal documents such as articles of incorporation and bylaws. However, there is still a chance that the condo association could become insolvent or even mismanage funds.

Another drawback that has to do with the condo association can be the poor management of properties. For instance, if a condo association is not doing its job well when it comes to maintaining the common areas, it can cause damage to the entire community. Since you are an owner, you will rely on the association to follow through their end of the bargain and do anything to maintain the value of your property. Their inability to manage the properties properly and make the needed upgrades to the building and to the community will affect the long-term appreciation of your property, making you lose quality tenants that would want to rent your unit.

As we have mentioned before, condo communities have rules that could both restrict and protect you. When it comes to limiting your freedom, condo rules can prevent you from renting out your unit. For example, most of the condo communities have a limit on the units that can be rented. If a tenant moves out, someone else rents another unit, and this limit is reached, you will not be able to rent your unit.

Another thing the condo association may limit is the length of the lease, the number of occupants, and various others that have to do with how you will be able to use your condo. With these policies, they aim for the prevention of turning the property into an apartment building rather than a community where owners reside. For you to be safe, you will have to make sure you will be able to rent your unit before you buy it and also secure that your tenants will be able to abide by the condo requirements. You can learn much information about the condo association from other tenants that live in a condo community. Ask them how it is like living there.

Townhouses

We can trace the origins of the modern townhouse back to early England when this term was linked to a property that a person had "in town". This type of real estate was usually owned by royalty or nobility since their main residence would normally be in the country. This term was maintained today and is used to include a wide range of residences and not as a home for only the wealthy. A townhouse is a single-family home that should share a wall with another house and have at least two floors. Each townhome is owned independently unlike a duplex or a fourplex and as the owner you will be able to rent it to others. Let us delve deeper into the pros and cons of owning a townhouse or else a townhome.

To start with, if you want to invest in a townhouse and later rent it or sell it, it is considered to be an affordable option when it comes to housing for families. After a quick research, you will discover that townhouses will be more popular in areas where the prices of buying or renting property are high and there are only little options of available land. There are places in the United States for example, where you will not see townhouses at all and you will see somewhere land is available.

Another benefit of investing in a townhouse is that you will be able to own the interior as well as the exterior of the building in contrast with investing in a condo. Even though townhouses are similar to condominiums, their main difference is that you own the exterior of the house. As we have analyzed, in condos, you will only own the interior of your unit.

There may be rules to follow which are determined by Homeowners Association as well as some added expenses to support the association, but its existence will be an added bonus for you to make sure that the value of your property will remain at high levels. Also, when your neighbors neglect to take care of their own property, Homeowners Association will be able to enforce certain rules that could include a foreclosure if they fail to comply. The expenses may be higher due to the association, but you will not see much difference from owning a single-family home with similar rules.

Added to the above benefits, you will be able to make your own decisions concerning your property. This is not true when it comes to owning a condominium, where stiff rules exist when it comes to the decisions you will be able to make for your property. For instance, when you own a condo, not being able to make decisions about the exterior of your home can be a considerable restriction for you and your tenant. Any replacement, upgrades, or maintenance work will be straight from the condo association and the bill will be sent straight to you for changes that were not yours. With townhouses, you will fully own the property and thus making the important decisions will be your responsibility concerning the necessary upgrades.

As for all maintenance expenses, when you own a townhouse you will not have to take them up completely on your own. With a single-family house, you will be totally alone when it comes to all the maintenance responsibilities, everything will have to go through your budget. Townhouses offer you a more lenient budget since there are some opportunities for you to save up costs. This is the case because you will be sharing one or two walls with your neighbors and thus there will be fewer expenses to consider. When you own a townhouse, your tenant will still be a part of a big community but without the restrictions of the condo association.

Due to the fact that more common areas with townhouse communities tend to be more available compared to other communities, you and your tenant will also be able to enjoy the benefits of having near a picnic area, an open space, and a playground, but keep in mind that those areas are shared within the community.

Also, you should consider the fact that townhouses tend to be faster to sell than other homes. When you invest in a townhouse, you are purchasing a property that will target two groups of potential buyers: families who wish to downsize and first-time owners. This translates to you being able to sell the property faster than you would if you owned a different unit. If you want to up the value of the townhome you purchase and later want to sell or rent, you could spend some time and money to soundproof your unit so as to avoid hearing any noise from the neighbors.

Since you will be living in a community, there will be common areas that will be accessible by everyone living there such as gardens, a small park, a lawn, or a playground under the responsibility of the association. However, if the townhouse has a back or front yard, it will be your or your tenant's responsibility to maintain it as well as the exterior of the house. But if your tenant likes to do work outside, mow the lawn, or create your own landscaping, this could be a problem for him or her. Most of the families living in townhouses prefer to have other people take care of these things for them since it allows them to spend more time with their families.

A townhouse will benefit greatly families, who lead a hectic lifestyle. For instance, new families will have multiple responsibilities varying from going back and forth to work, taking the kids to school and extracurricular activities, running errands, and struggling to find some family quality time to spend with each other. If you were to invest and rent a single-family house, your tenant would have to take out of his or her precious extra time to deal with the exterior chores. This problem will be solved by owning and renting out a townhouse.

Security is another benefit to consider when investing in a townhome. If your tenant or buyer needs to travel often due to the nature of his work or for family matters, then his house will not be left in the hands of burglars. For instance, single-family homes will require the tenant to hire someone to clean the pool or maw the lawn while he or she is away.

Also, the privacy of single-family homes can be seen as an invitation to burglars. When you or your tenant pays the fees of the association, then security is can be included in the benefits of investing in a townhome. When someone sees unknown people lurking around, they will take action to protect your property. Besides security, this could also apply to other things such as noticing a leaking roof faster or other maintenance related issues.

Finally, another benefit could be that most townhomes will allow your tenant to be closer to town. When it comes to single-family homes, they may be in a secluded area well into the country. Townhomes are most commonly found in the city or in the suburbs. This means that it will be easier to find a tenant because he or she will be closer to his or her work, near restaurants as well as other entertainment options and public transportation to lessen vehicle expenses.

Moving on to the disadvantages of investing in a townhome, the first one would be that townhouses are closely related to an apartment or a condo than a single-family home. This translates to seeing and hearing, especially if your walls are thin, your neighbors more often within this community. Even though the nature of townhomes can help you, your tenant or buyer be a part of a supportive and friendly community, the possibilities of having to deal with households that are not very friendly or concerned with maintaining the environment and their home clean are high.

Since you will own the townhouse for a while, this could affect the overall value of your property when you will wish to rent or sell it. To deal with this problem, you should first ask around and make a profile of the community the property you wish to buy is a part of.

When compared to a detached single-family home, the sense of privacy in a townhouse will be limited. This is a factor you tenant or buyer will have to consider. Another factor to consider is the sense of ownership in case you intend to sell or rent the property. Even though your buyer or tenant will have fewer maintenance chores to worry about, the fees paid to the association in order for them to maintain the common structures and areas may be high and in the long run your tenant or buyer will have to choose a single-family home to purchase or rent.

You will also have to pay monthly maintenance fees to the association and this happens for all townhomes and condos upon signing. The fee you may not expect is the one called the "capital contribution fee." This extra expense is paid at the transfer or the closing of the townhouse title. The amount varies and is based on the agreement, but it can usually be three times the monthly maintenance charge. The amount is assessed and consistent with the bylaws of the association your property belongs to. If this expense is not included in the MLS listing of your contract, you should ask about it before agreeing to purchase or sign anything binding.

Due to the fact that townhouses are commonly built in places of premium land, they usually stretch upward to have more space available. You may see a three-story or four-story unit with only one or two rooms on each floor. Such a design requires the usage of stairs often and thus it can pose a challenge for people who suffer from physical limitations. This option can be impractical for instance for families who have young children, people with disabilities, and the elderly. This problem can be solved if you talk before your purchase with the people living there and install an elevator system, however, keep in mind that there may not be enough room for you to do so.

From an investor's point, this could mean a loss of potential tenants or buyers since people will not be able to grow old in this home, for example. In other words, keep in mind that this is not always a solid investment when compared to a single-family home.

Another disadvantage can be the fact that townhouses do not appreciate fast when compared to other options you have in real estate. Even though you will find some exceptions to this rule, the norm is that most townhomes will not appreciate in value at the same pace a single-family home will. Also, if there is a housing bubble in the community you wish to make your investment at, the value will depreciate slower, but it cannot be considered as an investment where you will be able to make a lot of cash.

Added to the above disadvantages, you may have to respond to the complaints of neighbors as the owner about things that may be trivial, especially if you are renting this property you may also have to listen to your tenant complain about the neighbors. If you or your tenant fails to respond to complaints such as food smell, for instance, a lien will be placed on your home and thus you will b forced to make time to respond to complaints, even the ridiculous ones.

One last disadvantage of townhouses is the limited available storage options. For example, if your tenant or buyer wishes to fully decorate the property for each holiday or has kids with lots of toys and needs space for that entire plus two or three bicycles, a townhouse will not have, most times, the necessary storage or closet room for those things. You will need to have an offer prepared for an additional storage unit to satisfy the needs of your clients. In contrast, a single-family home will offer that additional storage room in the form of basement areas, a garage, and attic space. Townhomes usually will not even offer outdoor space for someone to store children's toys or stuff for your pet, things that larger families will typically need.

Cooperative Buildings

Moving on to the next type of residential type of property, cooperative buildings or else "co-ops" are defined as a unique form of housing option that can be found in limited numbers to the United States urban markets. Those forms of housing option first appeared in the United States in the late 1800s and rose in popularity in Washington DC in the 1920s. Nowadays cooperative buildings are very popular in Chicago.

To better understand the nature of a cooperative building, it is a property including many units that are owned by a company, most commonly a Limited-Liability Company (LLC). People who buy a unit in this building will turn into shareholders of the company that controls the property and attain exclusive leasehold of the unit they purchase. This means that the unit you will buy will be financed in the form of a home loan and not in the form of a residential mortgage since you will be buying shares in a company and not a real property.

The property that the company owns is managed by a cooperative building board consisting of a limited number of the shareholders, who are entrusted with making decisions that will benefit the corporation and thus other residents. This arrangement is different from a legal perspective than the one we analyzed with condos since, in the case of the condos; each unit has an individual owner.

The board of the cooperative building will get involved in all the purchases as well as sales by reviewing and approving all the applicants. Let us see the advantages and disadvantages of this arrangement.

In some cases, an advantage of this form of housing is the fact that cooperative buildings sometimes can be a less expensive option for housing. You will find them usually cheaper, in terms of per square foot than, for example, condos in the same area. Keep in mind that they also have low closing costs. When it comes to being in a high-cost housing market, cooperative buildings can be a long-term investment since a future sale of your unit can have as a result, important financial gains, despite the fact that the future owners will not be building equity.

When it comes to the disadvantages, owners will be able to not pay attention to chores relating to property management outside their units, but they will still have to pay a considerable amount of these expenses and due to the nature of ownership, the cost may be high. Also, when it comes to taxes, cooperative building owners will have to deal with different tax rules than homeowners who have mortgages. In the second group, those people will most commonly enjoy tax deductions. Added to this, if the board passes a major project for changes in the units, you will have to pay your part in it, even if you did not agree to the changes. Your part in these costs may be substantial.

When it comes to owning a unit in cooperative buildings, the board will have to approve of any new tenant and this includes the possibility of a new roommate. So, if you need to rent your unit, the new resident must be informed of those circumstances. As far as renovations are concerned, you may also need the approval of the board to make any changes to your unit. The approval for this may take a long time and it will most probably include an application fee. Another disadvantage can be the fact that you may not be able to rent your unit for a short time and if a tenant is not approved by the board, you will not be able to rent at all, even if you approve of him or her.

In addition to the above, if you are allowed to rent your unit, there are various co-ops that allow only a limited percentage of the unit to be leased and they may also ask for minimum residency that can typically be for up to three years before you will be able to make an approval application. When it comes to the approval of residents, in the United States cooperative boards must do so based on the Fair Housing Act. This act forbids discrimination based on national origin, sex, race, family status, religion, and disability. Those classes are protected by the government and states may have added classes based on marital status, height, source of income or sexual orientation.

Single Family Homes

Moving on, we will see the different benefits and drawbacks of investing in a single-family home. A single-family detached home is a structure in which one family is living and this structure is not attached to another building. Let us start by presenting the benefits of this investing choice.

The first benefit we could present to you is that tenants, in case of renting, will lease for longer than in the other cases of property investment. There are many single-family properties that are rented for one year and longer which is longer when compared to apartments or condos. Most families, who seek to rent a single-family home, usually want to save up and buy a new one. Keep in mind that the longer the leases last; they will increase the annual Return of Investment for you.

Another benefit of investing in a single-family home is that it holds its resale value, especially if it is maintained well and its location is ideal, for instance, in a thriving and well-reputed neighborhood. If those two requirements are met, your investment will almost certainly hold higher resale value. This is not true for neighborhoods that suffer from crime and declining economy since it will lose its value very quickly.

Also, detached single-family homes have lower annual property taxes when compared to multi-family homes or apartment buildings. Added to this, commercial real estate can be often taxed differently and taxes may be higher when compared to single-family homes. When it comes to costs, another benefit can be that single-family homes have lower management costs due to the fact that small families live inside. This is true especially when you have a tenant who will take excellent care of the house and thus lessen the costs of repairs that fall upon you with the renewal of each lease.

When it comes to the cons of investing in a single-family home, you should keep in mind that unlike multi-family homes, single-family homes are most commonly vacant the moment the lease ends. For this reason, you may have to budget for repairs after a vacancy, you will lose revenue from the times it stays vacant and your costs will be increased for finding a new tenant. Also, in most neighborhoods, the common property for an average single-family home is less than ¼ acre. Typically, families opt for renting a property with more land for convenience and this fact can translate into taking more time to find a new tenant to rent.

Last but not least, we have listed as a benefit the fact that single-family homes typically hold their resale value no matter how long before the property was constructed. This can be seen as a drawback too since the initial price of your investment will be high. When those homes are renovated before they are placed on the market, they will have a higher price for sale when compared to those that will need extra work for repairs during the time you will buy them.

Multi-Family Homes

The last type of residential property we are going to analyze is the multi-family home. Multi-family homes are properties designed to meet the needs and accommodate many families in various units inside the house. You will see these properties in many forms such as duplexes or triplexes as well as apartment buildings that can be considered multi-family homes. Many people consider them an investment choice but through the following analysis of pros and cons, you will be able to form a better opinion on whether this is the right investment for you.

One of the benefits of investing in multi-family homes is the number of money you will get by renting this property. By hosting many families in one property, your cash flow will increase, given the fact that each family will pay their part over the maintenance and ownership of the property. Each of the families living there will be a boost to your income, thus making single-family homes less profitable than the multi ones.

In terms of simplicity and convenience, a multi-family home will offer you the chance to deal with on mortgage instead of multiple ones that would be necessary to own multiple single-family homes. If you buy, for instance, a duplex with one mortgage you will have to deal with less paperwork and you will save more time than investing in more single-family homes. The same goes for insurance policies. When you own a multi-family home, you will have to deal with one insurance policy, even though it will be more expensive, you will not be open to multiple and different policies.

If you decide to invest in a multi-family home, you will mitigate your risk of being without tenants for a considerable amount of time and losing revenue. This is true because you will be dealing with three or more units, so the risk of a complete vacancy is not high. Even if you have one family move out, you will have other tenants to keep your revenues coming and maintain a positive level as you wait to fill the empty unit. Also, if the tenant of one unit delays in paying the rent, the other tenants can make up for the lost time.

Also, the competition for renting and purchasing single-family homes is considerably high because it is considered to be an easy way to enter the area of real estate investing. For this reason, if you choose to invest in multi-family homes, you will have less competition in terms of biding for rent and purchases. Added to this, the price of single-family homes is most commonly based on which house families find appealing, which is often based on different neighborhoods and the changes within them. On the other hand, multi-family homes are priced based on the potential they have to generate income for the investor. They are considered primarily as a form of investment and for this reason, they are bought and sold, so they have more stable growth in the long term.

Moving on to the downsides of investing in a multi-family property, the first one would be the price they are sold at. They are more expensive than single-family homes. Even though you will not be required to pay for a double price when it comes to a duplex one, if you aim to invest in homes with more than three units, prices can be very high. If you are low on cash and this is your first investment in properties, multi-family homes may be too expensive for you to consider.

Also, by owning a multi-family property, you will need to make room for more management time since each unit in the house will result in more responsibilities when it comes to management and more time to be spent for you taking up the role of a landlord. You will have to deal with many tenants at the same time, different sets of appliances, and different schedules. Not to mention that if something breaks in the property it will affect many other units at once and thus making the repair bills larger.

When we analyzed the pros of investing in a multi-family property, we mentioned that you will have fewer competitors to deal with when compared to single-family properties. However, the type of competition will change. Due to the advantages and nature of multi-family property investing, these units tend to be the targets of experienced investors with many more years of experience on their backs than you have. This can result in you finding difficult searching for tenants as well as pricing your units the right way.

Another thing you should keep in mind is that multi-family properties are typically more complicated than single-family homes. For example, if you end up with a tenant that causes trouble, all the other tenants are going to suffer from it or if you end up with a structural damage, the price of your property will fall considerably. Also, multi-family homes are not that freely available, including those who are lower in demand, than single-family homes. This translates to you facing some difficulties finding the perfect property for your needs since your options will be limited.

One last drawback of multi-family homes is that you will have to research the various regulations about how you will be able t rent your property. This includes the laws of your state so as to not risk imprisonment or paying fines for not abiding by the rules. Keep in mind that rules for multi-family homes are stricter than those who govern single-family properties. Even though multi-family homes can be very profitable, they are also very challenging and complicated.

Now that we have seen the various residential properties you can invest in, let us see the different investment strategies you can apply to your investing career and make reliable as well as profitable choices.

Real Estate Investing Strategies

It is true that the real estate market can be deemed as intimidating by some people. However, it is not a faraway dream for people and like everything else you need to know a few things before you get yourself involved. For instance, the golden rule of real estate investment is location. Location is the first thing to consider when you want to choose a property to invest in.

For example, college towns demand rental property. Even though, in this case, you might be afraid to rent your property at a crazy college kid that will make more harm than good, there are many professors or graduate students as well as support staff that will need to rent a house in a college town. To be on the safe side you could protect your real estate investment, in such a case, with checking your potential tenant's financial statements, references, or credit checks.

You could also try to invest in a property that is close to the area you are living, let us say thirty minutes from where your house. This has some appeal since you will know the area well and you will be able to respond quickly to problems that have to do with your property instead of hiring someone to do it for you. However, there are also some disadvantages that have to do with the fact that you may not be able to afford to invest in property of your local area or that you may not be able to purchase as many properties as you would like given the prices. Also, if your area gets hit by an economic slump or a natural disaster occurs, your properties will be vulnerable since they will all be around the same place.

When you are searching for properties to buy, there are various aspects you have to think of apart from the economic picture of the area you are searching at. For example, is this area visited or filled with younger people? Young people are more likely to rent than older people since they move around more. They want to live in central places, preferably in cities with lots of events, a certain culture, a good bar, and a good restaurant. Also, a considerable percentage of people do not own cars, so they will choose to live in cities that are friendly to bicycles, are walkable, and have an easy transportation system. Apart from that, you should also check the crime rate of the area you wish to invest in. No one will want to live in a neighborhood where crime is an everyday occurrence. In order for you to be certain about such things, you could read the local newspapers, ask around or look at a crime map.

Another factor to consider when you wish to enter the real estate market is how much money you are able to spend. The answer to this part will depend greatly on whether you are able to pay with cash if you have to take a mortgage. For both options, there are benefits and drawbacks to consider.

When you are able to pay with cash, you will be able to avoid the mortgage process and thus you will not have to pay interests. Also, if you are able to make an offering for a property in cash, you may take many steps ahead of your competition since sellers like cash payments. However, if you have a limited amount of cash you are able to invest, paying with this method is not the ideal choice since it will tie your hands in one asset and you will not be diversified.

When it comes to leveraging or else mortgaging, there are several financial sites that recommend this choice as the best one since the investor will be able to have the cash to invest in various assets and achieve diversification. This way you will be able to buy more than one property and you can make sure that your money will be invested in more than one property and be open to possibly different markets if your properties are in different cities.

However, if the real estate market went into a crisis mode and the values of the properties declined sharply, you will be in a position where you are going to owe more money than the house itself is worth. To lessen the risks involved, it would be good if you did your homework beforehand when it comes to the different mortgage terms offered that will best suit you and the properties you wish to invest in.

Another rule that many real estate investors follow is the 1% rule. This simple rule states that the monthly rent of a property should be equal or greater than 1% of the value of the home you purchased in order for you to get the best return of investment. For instance, if you purchased a property for $100.000, your rent should be $1.000 per month. If the amount of rent is less than what your research on other houses in the area has shown, the selling price of the home is probably overpriced. This rule will not tell you everything and you don't have to adhere to it without a thought, but it is a good starting point and a nice way to assess the long list of properties you are assessing as your future real estate investments.

Added to the above, if you are new to the area of real estate investing and you have never owned your own home, you probably are not aware of the various things to look for about the different problems or the things that could cause problems within a home. To solve this problem, you could hire a home inspector who has about 1.600 items on his or her list of things to watch out for, maybe even more.

If your home inspector does find problems, you could start negotiations with the seller to fix the issues the inspector pointed out or to reduce the price of the property so as for you to fix those problems yourself. Keep in mind that the home inspector may find so many problems with the house that you will have to pass on the purchase of this particular property.

For instance, a home inspector may look at the age of the roof; list all the cracks on the home foundations, note the exterior condition, and search for any signs of water damage. For this reason, a home inspection is not the thing to cut off your list if you want to save money. If this step is passed, then you will have to pay double the amount of purchase to make this house livable for others to rent.

Another golden rule of real estate investing is for the investor to have an emergency fund for his or her rental property. This step will not only protect the investment you will make, but it will also keep you at peace. An emergency fund will include money sealed in a savings account to be used for unexpected expenses and routine repairs such as fixing various small damages in between tenants or replacing a roof after a natural disaster occurs.

A common method followed by mortgage lenders is for a buyer to have saved at least 6 months' worth of mortgage payments before the loan is given. However, if the home you want to invest in is older and for this reason, will need more repairs compared to a new property, you will most likely have to increase that amount. That number should also be higher when the history of this property indicates, long times of vacancies between tenants.

There is a lot of work involved in real estate investment and not only for finding the right house to invest in and in the right place that will offer you more revenues. For instance, you have to advertise your property and be able to respond to maintenance problems, deal with cases of eviction and collect the rent, not to mention the construction of the lease. Then, you need to be prepared to make all these things again when a tenant moves out. If you are not able to do all these things by yourself you may have to hire a property management company.

You could also create a team, instead of hiring a property management company, that will help you through this process, especially if you aim to purchase and own more properties than one or two. For you to make the best team is the reputation each person has. Some suggestions of positions that you need to fill for your team are a real estate agent, a property manager, and a home inspector.

To have a better understanding of how you could make money from real estate investing, there are various strategies to consider as a new investor. Think of the process you are going to follow as the mountain that is real estate investing and the careful climber that is you, the investor. In order for you to reach the top, which is your life and financial goals, you will have to go through several sub-goals before you achieve your main one.

Strategies are as useful as the map of a mountain is. They show you the different routes you will have to take in order to reach the peak safely and quickly. Strategies also include tactics that can be viewed as the necessary tools for you to climb to that mountain following the route you chose. However, before you consider which tactics are best, you should get clear on your goal for investing in real estate such as financial freedom, then pick one or two strategies that fit your needs and then get clear on the tactics.

Due to the variety of strategies available for real estate investors, we are going to follow a model where strategies are divided into groups based on the end result they provide. For example, the first group of real estate investing strategies we are going to present, are business strategies. Strategies of real estate investing under the category of business strategies are viewed as a way to develop your own business rather than make some investments. In other words, your investments will grow to generate income that will be able to support all your needs and could replace your job. However, if you choose to follow the strategies included in this group, you must be prepared to invest not only money but a lot of effort and time during your business start-up in order to be successful.

Fix-and-Flip

The first strategy of the business group is the Fix-and-Flip one. According to this strategy, the investor will have to follow a business path of searching for properties that need work including doing all the necessary repairs and then selling them again at a higher price to make a profit. By following this model, your aim will be to make money in order to generate savings for your future investments and pay the bills. Renovating the houses you purchase will not be an easy job, but the later selling price will make all your efforts worth it.

Flipping a property is admittedly a riskier investment than rental properties and as is the case with every risky business the rewards can be immense if all your plans are safely carried out or it could turn into a disaster if your plans fail. One of the benefits of flipping a property is the considerable potential you have to achieve a quick profit. Most investors who opt for real estate flip are hoping to make money faster than in other real estate investing methods. Also, with this method, you will be able to gain experience in various areas that will later help you with building your future in real estate investing.

For instance, you will gain experience and learn more about construction. If you follow real estate flip you will need to take care of the remodeling, the renovation, and repairing of the properties you purchase. This will offer you insight into different areas of construction. You will be able to understand, after a certain point, how much different materials cost as well as the various electrical and plumbing repairs. You will also be able to do to a certain degree the job of a property inspector by spotting big issues each house has on its structure and environment such as asbestos and mold. As you delve deeper and carry out more projects, through this construction experience you will be able to recognize the various ways you could generate more money on future projects since you will know how to seal the best budget deal.

Also, you will learn how to conduct a market research. Always before making a purchase for a house to flip, you should conduct market research to look for the best deals you can make. For example, you could talk to real estate brokers in the area you look to purchase, look for "for sale" advertisements, and search for houses that have been recently sold to get a better idea on the selling prices as well as what people are looking for in a house in that area.

Market research is essential because you have to know your target audience. For example, in one part of a country, people would want a modern house design while in another part; buyers will opt for a more traditional house design. Your renovation goals should be similar to the demand of the market of your choice, otherwise, you will have to sell the renovated house at a lower price or even worse not be able to sell it at all.

You will instantly gain more experience the moment you place the first property you flipped up for sale. This is true because you will have a better insight into the various things buyers are searching for in the are of your first sale. It would be best if you kept notes on what buyers liked or did not like to make the necessary changes in your following projects. Another thing you will learn about this type of property investment with your first flip are the unexpected costs. It would be better for everyone, especially investors if everything went according to plan, however, you'd be surprised at how many times this does not happen.

Every investment has risks and this is why it is necessary to learn how to mitigate risks. This includes the unexpected costs that will come your way. Through experience, you will learn how to plan expenses for contractor disputes, construction delays, building permits, delays in delivery materials, and keeping up with the costs of when you are not able to sell your property as quickly as you had initially planned.

Also, another benefit of this real estate investment strategy is that you will increase your network. Throughout every flipping project, you will make new contacts in the industry such as building inspectors, real estate brokers, other investors, attorneys, insurance brokers, and contractors. These contacts will be useful for any future investment you will make, so try to be at your best behavior and always be professional when you are dealing with such people.

Last but not least, you will feel proud because you will be able to see the potential of a property that others will not be able to. This is an advantage of a real estate flip that can also be developed through experience. You have a vision that can increase the value of a home when others thought it was merely useless and with no value.

On the other hand, there are several disadvantages to consider with this method of real estate investing. The main one is the risk of losing large sums of money instead of making large sums of money. There are various factors that can lead to this worst-case scenario such as:

- ✓ Unexpected costs: Even though you will learn in time how to control the various sources where unexpected costs come from, unanticipated costs such as contractor delays, permit delays, material delays, building permits and renovations you had not planned, can add up very quickly and lead you to make no profits.

✓ High taxes: Once the renovations you had planned for your property are complete, the city may choose to increase the taxes you will have to pay for your property. As a result, you will probably face many difficulties finding a buyer and thus be forced to pay those taxes yourself and even if you find one, the added taxes may make him rethink buying your property.

✓ Other costs: If you have a mortgage on the property, you will have to pay for it even after the renovations are complete. Also, you will have to pay the insurance and taxes on the property for the period of time you will own it. These are costs that will take a large sum out of your budges and the costs will be greater the longer the ownership stays in your hands. Another thing to consider is the maintenance costs since the yard will have to be cleaned, as well as the snow, and the grass will have to be cut.

Selling difficulties: In real estate investing and especially for this strategy, you lose money for each day you cannot find a buyer to sell your property due to the fact that you will have to pay for the costs of holding the property. Also, for the longer, the property remains available in the market, the likelihood of having to reduce the selling price, which will be a hit to your expected profits.

Another drawback of this real estate strategy is the stress associated with it. You will have to find the right property, plan properly for all the costs involved and deal with contractors. Stress is something you will have to learn to control in the long run, but at first, it will be there.

Wholesaling

Another real estate investment strategy is wholesaling. Wholesaling is defined as the business when an investor finds good deals of properties and then resells them almost instantly with a small heightened price. In order for you to be good at this business you have to develop negotiating and marketing skills in order to be able to fish those good deals. For this business, you also have to like sales and be good at them. If this is true then you will be good at wholesaling. However, if you hate sales, you must choose a different real estate investment strategy.

This type of strategy is one of the perfect choices for investors who want to make profits from short-term investments. The process that is usually followed is:

- ✓ Finding a property for sale
- ✓ Having the property for sale under contract
- ✓ Selling the property to another investor

Due to the fact that a wholesale real estate investor does not keep the properties, he or she invests in or holds them for using them as rental properties, wholesaling in real estate is deemed as short-term investments. Let us see the steps to be followed in wholesaling real estate.

In the wholesale real estate investment strategy, the first step is to find a property up for sale. Keep in mind that not any property that is up for sale will be ideal for a wholesale investor. The properties that will do the job will be priced below market value or have motivated sellers, as is called in the real estate world. Motivated sellers are the ones who are willing to sell a real estate investment at a lower price. Let us see the different ways you will be able to find such a property for sale that fits the wholesaling real estate definition:

- ✓ With comparative market analysis: It will determine if the property is sold below market value.
- ✓ By developing a real estate network to discover motivated sellers.
- ✓ With indulging in real estate investment marketing.

Through a visit to the city hall of the area you want to invest in. There, you will find a list of properties available in the real estate market that are believed to be fixer-upper investment properties or are near to foreclosure.

The next step to this strategy is to place the property for sale under contract. Once you find the appropriate property for sale, which is below market value or you negotiated with a motivated seller for a reduced price, you will have to pay for a wholesale real estate contract. This will cost you approximately $10.

The last step of this investment strategy is for you to sell the property to another real estate investor. It would be wise for you to already have searched and find the real estate investor before you even make the offer for the property that is for sale. This way, you will have a guarantee that your property will be sold quickly. A common practice amongst real estate investors is to buy low and sell high. However, this is not the case for a wholesale investor who buys low and also sells the property for a low price. This happens because the new buyer must have a good return on his or her investment.

Let us see an example to better understand this strategy. If you, as a wholesaler, find a property that is worth $150.000 after the necessary repairs are made, you managed to negotiate the price down to $125.000. So, a good price for this property, after the contract is made, will be $140.000. This way, the wholesale investor will profit and the buyer will be able to make a good return of investment after he or she makes additional repairs.

The above is the most basic form of wholesaling in real estate. You are probably able to understand the pros and cons of the above analysis, but let us delve deeper into them. To start with, one of the main benefits of this investing model is that it does not require a cash investment. You will have no down payments, no credit score review, and no monthly mortgage payments.

Another benefit will be that this way is the faster path to make money through real estate investing. This is one of the reasons why many investors of this field chose wholesaling real estate because they are able to make quick money from it. If you manage to find properties that are sold below market value, you will be able to sell it quickly to a real estate investor due to the positive return of investment you are able to bring on the table.

Even though it may take you some time to discover properties for sale with such requirements as well as the real estate investors to buy them, you will typically be done with a property in a matter of a few months. You will probably be wondering why wholesaling is considered one of the fastest methods to make money in real estate and the answer will be because you will not have to wait for rental income, checks, and for all the renovations to be over.

Wholesaling is also recommended for beginners in real estate investing because there is no cash investment involved and not much experience is needed for you to follow this strategy. Also, through research and good planning, there is little risk involved, something that helps beginners move forward in this field of investing. Wholesaling real estate can be a great opportunity to learn all you need to know about real estate investing in a relatively safe manner. You will be able to develop necessary skills such as negotiating the price of a property, to find properties that are sold below market value and recognize the specific points of a good deal. Added to this, you will be able to create a good real estate network through this method that will later help you if you wish to switch strategies.

An important benefit we briefly mentioned before is the low risk involved in such an investment. Investments that are low on risks are always chaced by real estate investors because it is not as easy as many would think to find low-risk investments in the real estate market. Beginners should always watch out for investment opportunities and grasp every chance they can get their hands on to make a good deal through negotiation. In other words, wholesaling is considered to be a low-risk investment because the amount of cash that is at stake is not that much when compared to the losses of other real estate investment strategies.

Moving on to the drawbacks of wholesale real estate investing the first one would be that there is no guarantee on regular income. This means that there are high chances of wholesale real estate investing not being able to replace your full-time job since once the property is purchased, it will not make you any more money. On the other hand, rental properties will benefit you in having a stable income that real estate investors will be able to rely on.

Also, the fact that wholesale real estate investments are considered to be an easy and quick way of making money in this field, it does not mean that you will not have to dedicate a considerable amount of effort. Until you gain the necessary experience of finding properties priced below market value as well as the investors that wish to buy from you, those steps can cause you a lot of trouble and effort in wholesaling real estate investing. Networking is essential and it cannot be done in a matter of a few days.

You need to be dedicated and learn everything you can lay your hands on finding the appropriate properties for investing, the right sellers that are willing to reduce the price of the property you are interested in as well as the right buyers. Once you have learned how wholesaling real estate investing works, you will be a successful real estate investor.

The following three strategies we are going to present are considered to be the safest when someone wants to start in real estate investing and there are even some cases where little work is required as well as a considerably small amount of cash. Let us see those strategies in more detail.

House Hacking

When the term house hacking is used, it refers to someone who lives in a home that can produce income for this person. Such houses can be a triplex, duplex, fourplex, and generally houses that have extra space which can be rented like spare bedrooms, guest house, or a basement. It is considered to be another great way to invest in real estate because by renting your extra space, you will be able to reduce your housing costs. For instance, you can rent your space to a person that will, in turn, pay off your mortgage. This strategy is different than other traditional ways of investing in real estate because you are living in the property you invest in.

An example of house hacking can be the following. You can buy a four-unit property and reside in one of the four units. Then, you will be able to rent the other three in order to cover your monthly mortgage costs. This property is considered to be occupied by the owner due to the fact that you are living in one of the units. For this reason, you will be able to be financed through mortgages easier, but the interest rate may be a bit increased due to the risk of owning a property with many units.

Continuing with our example, let us assume that your fees per month for housing are $2.000, if you are able to rent the three remaining units for $750 per month, your monthly rent will reach in total $2.250. To translate the numbers, with $2.250 you will be covering your monthly fees and then have $150 leftover for your needs. This is an example of how house hacking works.

You will still have to pay for the upkeep and the maintenance of the property as well as for the times the other units or rooms stay vacant if tenants move out or if they refuse to pay. This is the risk of house hacking. You will have no guarantee that your tenants will pay and you are going to make a profit out of renting your spare space. This could result in your inability to pay your monthly mortgage. However, if it does work you will be able to make money monthly and live for free without having to worry about making ends meet to pay your mortgage.

Now that we have explained better how house hacking works, let us take a better look at the pros and cons of this real estate investment strategy. The obvious benefit we stressed before is that you will have an extra income to pay your mortgage each month instead of having to pay it on your own. Also, you will have reduced housing expenses, since the person you are letting live in your extra space will have to contribute to the house bills every month. This can be applied to utilities such as phone, cable, water, gas, internet, electric, etc. You will split those bills evenly for the other tenants to pay too.

The main drawback of house hacking as a real estate investment is that your home is not really yours. If you are residing in a property with many units, you will be able to place some space between you and your tenants. However, if you have a single-family house, you will share many rooms with those you are renting your space to and that could result in various awkward and even annoying situations. Also, things could get serious if they fail to pay their rent on time or if they want you to do them a "favor". Not to mention the danger of your tenants damaging your units.

To sum up, here is a list of the various ways you can follow the house hack strategy for real estate investing:

- ✓ Purchase a multi-unit property and reside in the units that are not for rent.
- ✓ Rent an empty room at your single-family house.
- ✓ Reside in the guesthouse and rent your main home.

- ✓ Rent all of the rooms of your house and live in the garage or sleep on the couch.
- ✓ Place your house for rent through Airbnb.

Live-In Home Flipping

The live-in home flipping strategy has to do with you buying and living into a house, making the necessary renovations to fix it up and wait for approximately two years or more to sell it and make a profit. You can buy one of the ugliest homes that are located in some of the best neighborhoods and spend the next few years to fix it up. By waiting two years to resell it, you will get out of paying considerable amounts of cash in taxes for the profit. For instance, an individual would reach up to $250.000 and for a couple of $500.000.

The above is one of the most obvious benefits of live-in house flipping. You will be exempt from having to pay capital gain taxes on the sale of the property if you have resided in the house for at least two out of five years. With this real estate investing strategy, you will not have to buy a property and then sell it very fast. For this reason, you will not have to acquire two mortgages since you can take your time to sell the home.

Given the time you will have to reside in the home you will later sell, you can save up money from construction if you do some of the work yourself. If you know a thing or two about fixing a house, you will be able to buy a house that is not in the best condition since they are cheaper than relatively newly constructed ones. However, do some research on this matter because some locales require you to hire a professional. There are many cases of people who followed this real estate investing strategy and had to budget only for raw materials to renovate the house.

Another benefit of this strategy is that you will be able to use an owner-occupied mortgage financing. As an investor, you will have to place at least 20% down for an investment home mortgage with probably higher interest rates. This is not the case with owner-occupied mortgages.

One of the drawbacks of this strategy is that you will have to move around a lot if you want to make considerable profits that are tax-free. Your home will also turn into a construction zone. So, if you have a thing for extreme cleanliness and can't bear the thought of having dust lying in your house, this is not the real estate investing strategy for you. Also, if you are used to having many people over you house for entertainment purposes, you will have to stop or lessen the visits considerably. Another thing you have to keep in mind is that you may have to get used to having workers around the house all the time. They may use inappropriate language you don't want your children to hear, they may use your bathroom, or play music higher than the volume of your preference. Those are things you should consider before making the decision to follow this strategy.

Added to the above, your free time will lessen considerably, especially if you choose to save up costs by doing various repairs to the house yourself. Last but not least, the fact that you will live in the house first, renovate it, and then sell it, does not mean that you should not place any thought on which property will sell. You still have to watch out for basic things like what buyers want in the area you wish to buy a property and then renovate it accordingly.

BRRRR Investing

The BRRRR investing term stands for Buy, Rehab, Rent, Refinance, Repeat. This strategy has to do with an investor pulling capital out of a property so that he or she can invest it in another property. This real estate investing strategy will seem to people searching which path to choose to invest in real estate as a nearly certain way to be able to make money. This strategy is presented as a formula and there is a common belief that as long as you follow this formula, you will not risk losing. However, you should keep in mind that there are no guarantees and there is always a risk to be considered, even with BRRRR.

With this method, you should essentially lookout for fixer-up properties to purchase bellow their full value. Then, you have to repair them, lease them to reliable tenants, and refinance to get your money back. Then, you should repeat the process over again.

Probably the most important step in this strategy is to buy a property with a smart deal. By making a smart deal we mean that the property should be at a great neighborhood and a great location. The BRRRR investing strategy may seem to you similar to the house flipping one we previously mentioned. This may be true because it essentially is house flipping, but instead of selling the house you purchase, you will have to rent it after renovating it. The same ideas that we analyzed in house flipping are applied here too.

One of the benefits of this strategy is the great return on investment since your initial investment comes from the money you will pull out of the first property you invested in. In order for you to plan accordingly and achieve the best return on investment is to seal a successful real estate rehab. The first step to do this is to inspect the property well. After you buy a fixer-upper, go through a home inspection with a qualified inspector. The inspector should assess the rehab house from roof to basement. Let us see a list of what you should check:

- ✓ Air conditioning
- ✓ Furnaces
- ✓ Roof
- ✓ Plumbing
- ✓ Roof
- ✓ Windows
- ✓ Water issues in the basement
- ✓ Flooring

Then, you should create a scope of work for your contractors to have a better idea about the level of your project for the rehab of the property. The scope of work should include all the repairs and renovations needed, even the small ones. It should also include the costs you have estimated for each project including any demolitions, removals, and installations.

Your next step should be to hire a contractor and be certain you choose correctly because a contractor will either break or make your real estate rehab project. You will be able to find a reliable and qualified contractor through websites, job boards, local real estate associations, and local supply houses. However, do not think that the only thing you have to do is approach him or her and hire him instantly. You need to make a document that includes information about yourself, the scope of your project, your goals for this project, your pay schedules, and the different things you demand of the contractor. With this move, you will be able to attract the right contractors and show them that you are an investor that can be trusted. Below is a list of things that contribute to the assessment of a contractor and will help you conduct the appropriate interviews:

- ✓ Insurances
- ✓ How many workers he or she has in his or her team
- ✓ The equipment they own

- ✓ Years of experience
- ✓ Permits and licenses
- ✓ Subcontractors
- ✓ Willing to offer referrals
- ✓ Any bankruptcies

After you are done with the interviews, you should request them to send their offers for your project. Assess every bid carefully along with the information you have gathered during the interviews. This is an important part of your project since you trust someone to carry out your future investment.

Once you have hired the contractor that best suits your needs, you will have to start working on the necessary paperwork. Keep in mind that your project should start when both parties have signed all the paperwork required. Let us see what such paperwork should include:

- ✓ Scope of work
- ✓ Insurance indemnification form
- ✓ Independent contractor agreement
- ✓ Payment information

After that step, you should watch out because you may need permits from the local authorities before you start your renovation project on your investment property. Let us see a list of the possible permits you may need:

- ✓ Cutting trees
- ✓ Upgrading or installing an electrical box
- ✓ Altering or moving a load-bearing wall
- ✓ Adding doors or windows to your house
- ✓ Changing the plumbing
- ✓ Working at a public sewer line
- ✓ Placing a new roof to the house

In order to make sure of the permits you may need, you have to visit your local authority. If you move to the renovations you have planned without the needed permit, you endanger yourself to get fined or demolish the renovations you have already completed.

The next step will be to manage the work conducted at your investment property which includes several stages that are very important. Some of them are:

- ✓ Electricity
- ✓ Plumbing
- ✓ Cleaning up the trash
- ✓ Demolition
- ✓ Insulation

✓ Painting and trimming

When the work is done, you must conduct an inspection to make sure the contractor you hired was able to complete all the renovations you have listed in your agreement. If everything is well and you are happy with the end result, you will have to ask the contractor to sign the final waiver of lien. Then, you can make the end payment and take full ownership of your property.

The final state will be renting out or sell your investment property after months of renovations and repairs. You should make sure that the bathroom, kitchen, living room, master bedroom, as well as the exterior of the home are presentable and able to convince people to buy or rent your investment property in order to sell or rent quickly. Also, if you wish to rent your property, you should take photos of your investment property and choose a well-visited website to make sure that you find a tenant quickly and start generating your income.

Those were a few major strategies to follow that could help you when you make your first steps on real estate investing. Each of the strategies presented has risks in them since no path is clear of danger. The key is to learn how to recognize the risks and take the necessary measures to contain them or be well-prepared to handle the consequences.

The Major Risks Involved in Real Estate Investing

No one can deny the fact that real estate investing can be one of the best ways for people to make money and built their wealth. The benefits of buying and being the owner of investment properties are many and one of the most important ones is acquiring a passive income from rental properties. Even though owning a rental property is considered to be a somewhat safe way to invest in real estate, not every real estate investor will be able to attain a risk-free success in such a competitive market.

Real estate investments, just like any other type of investment, have risks involved. Part of the job of a real estate investor, no matter the level of experience he or she has, is to be aware of them and learn how to avoid them by finding the perfect rental property in order to succeed in this business. Let us analyze some of the major risks involved in real estate investing.

The first risk we will analyze is the unpredictability that governs the real estate market. Despite the economic crises, the real estate market has grown well in the few years that have passed. However, there is no assurance that this will continue to be the case. The ups and downs of the real estate market are known by everyone along with the changing economic situation local or global. The economy has an essential role in the real estate market since it will determine the value of an investment property. As a result, you will not be guaranteed a profit whenever you make the important decision to invest in real estate.

Let us see an example to better understand this risk. Let's say you decide to purchase an investment property when the demand for real estate investing is high. Then, you are risking selling your investment property at a lower price than the money you paid for it during purchase, even if the property is used to generate profit through rent. This will happen due to the fact that as the real estate market changes, its value has dropped. As a result, this will cost you money, more money than you have earned while you rented out your investment property.

To learn how to deal with this risk, as a real estate investor, you should make the necessary research before you even enter the market on how this dynamic works. You need to understand how the market economy functions and works and be updated for all the new trends and future predictions. This way, you will be able to plan ahead and eventually learn how to predict the downturns of the market. As a result, you will know whether or not the time is right to buy an investment property and thus make a great investment decision.

Another risk real estate investors should be aware of is choosing the right location for your property. It is a known fact that location is everything in real estate investing. Real estate investors that are at the top of their field agree that location should be a top factor to consider when you make the decision to buy any type of investment property. You may wonder why location is so important and is considered a very important risk when it comes to real estate investing. The answers vary because a bad location will result in a failed investment in several ways.

For instance, the location of your investment property will determine the demand and supply. You may make the decision to purchase an investment property in a particular location due to its low price and also think that your decision is the right one. However, such locations may have many investment properties for sale and not bought due to them lacking a good job market and a growing population. By taking into consideration just these two factors, making an investment to such a location will be filled with risks for real estate investors because their properties will be harder to sell or rent.

Also, this area may have problems with crime and thus the investment properties are priced less. Would you buy or rent a property where you are in constant danger of being robbed? The crime rate in a location is an extremely important factor to consider when you are searching for properties to invest in. However, such areas may have a high occupancy rate due to the fact that people often tend to rent homes instead of buying them and the low rent can be an attractive deal for some tenants. But when an investor decides to purchase property in areas with a high crime rate, he is placing his or her property at risk of being robbed or vandalized which in turn will result in having unplanned expenses for high repair costs.

Another way location affects your profits is through appreciation. The location of an investment property is able to determine appreciation. Real estate properties, over time, tend to appreciate or else increase in value, unlike computers, cars, or boats. If the appreciation is low, it results in a negative return on investment during the time where the investor makes the decision to sell his or her investment property. For this reason, real estate investors should never purchase investment properties based only on their price.

You could avoid this risk, by always researching the location and choose the best one that is appropriate for real estate investing. Even though cheap deals may have a certain appeal, the risks that come after are not worth it. When we talk about location in real estate, we refer to the country, city, state, street, neighborhood, or even the exact address. The perfect location will be the one that will bring to the investor the highest return on investment. You want to buy an investment property in a location that is high in demand and low on rental properties. A location where rents are high and with reasonable property prices. This location should also be safe so as for the tenants not to damage your investment property beyond repair. But how do you choose such a location?

You will need to do a lot of research by reading various real estate investing resources. You could start by learning about the state of the national real estate market and later focus on the specific areas you are interested in. Those areas should be the ones that appear to perform better than other locations at the moment. When you have selected some locations that interest you, keep researching on the markets of those locations, the surrounding areas, and their inhabitants. For instance, you should check if people there are renting or are homeowners and if the area is safe to live in. You should also check about the location's public transportation, roads, hospitals, and all the various things that would convince people to rent or buy a property in the area.

Another risk that we are going to analyze is the negative cash flow. When we mention a negative cash flow of an investment property we refer to the amount of money, translated into profit, the investor earns after he or she has paid off al taxes, expenses, and mortgage payments. When you invest in a property you aim for positive cash flow, not a negative one which will be translated in the expenses paid for mortgage payments, expenses, and taxes are higher than the income generated by the investment property. As a result of the negative cash flow, you will be losing money. An investor has a higher chance of developing negative cash flow when he buys investment properties without first carrying out a real estate market analysis.

As a result, you will be able to avoid this risk by making sure you have calculated your income and your expenses, like how much you will receive from rent and how much money you will have to spend on your investment property before buying it. The location of your investment property will also help you in achieving a positive cash flow. You need to make sure it is on a prime location to accomplish a high return on investment. When it comes to real estate investing it would be wise for you to be as accurate when calculating your expenses and revenues as possible. Even the little expenses you disregarded first may add up and cause you problems in the long run.

Keep in mind that when you buy an investment property, there is no guarantee of quick profits or that in the case you rent your investment property you will have no vacancy related problems. So, the next risk an investor should watch out for is the risk of vacancy. There may come a time when you will have to face a high vacancy rate, which will pose a serious problem to your rental income since it can bring about negative cash flow. Especially when investors rely solely on rental income and tenants are the source for it, they are at risk of failing to pay off their insurance, property taxes, mortgage, and other related expenses.

Location plays an important role in controlling the risk of vacancy too. Investors should buy an investment property in a reputable location which is high in demand. Such locations have a working transportation system, safe neighborhoods, schools, and shopping malls.

On the subject of rental real estate investing, tenants are necessary for making money. However, not every tenant available will do the job to guarantee profits to the investor. The risk of ending up with bad tenants and being stuck with them could be considered as an even great risk than having an empty investment property. Even though having a vacant investment property means no profits at all, bad tenants may cause more problems by refusing to pay the rent for many months in a row and damage the property too much. As a result, you will have to deal with evictions, a process that is very expensive and time-consuming. To avoid this risk, you should select your tenants carefully by conducting interviews, checking their credit score and even ask to contact their previous landlord.

Hidden structural problems are another common risk, real estate investors have to deal with. They may end up purchasing an investment property filled with serious hidden structural problems and as a result, the costs of maintenance and unexpected repairs will rise considerably. To avoid having to deal with this risk, you should evaluate carefully the state of your investment property and get a home appraisal before even buying the property. Property appraisers will be able to detect any hidden problems or damages that need to be fixed since they are professionals. Also, they will be able to tell you how much your investment property will cost in case you decide to buy it.

Real estate investors often come across the risk of low liquidity. Real estate investing has to do with investment properties that are illiquid. When we talk about liquidity we refer to the ability of an investor to have immediate access to money they have placed in an investment. Illiquid investments such as investment properties, will not offer the investor the ability to convert them easily into cash. You may think that selling the investment property will resolve this issue, but it is not a quick or easy process. If there is a haste to sell the investment property it will result in considerable losses of your investment since you will have to sell at a lower price.

Foreclosure is another risk real estate investors have to plan for. When investors are not able to pay off their mortgage payments for a few months in a row, they are at risk of losing their investment property to the bank, in other words, they are at risk of foreclosure. When dealing with a foreclosure, you will probably lessen your chances of getting approval for future bank loans. The best way for you to avoid this foreclosure risk is to conduct an investment property analysis and a real estate market analysis before you decide to pay the 20% down payment for your investment property. You should also have an emergency fund aside to pay off your mortgage as quickly as possible.

In real estate investing, the value of a property is expected to rise over the years. This process is called appreciation. However, this is not a guarantee for all properties and the risk of depreciation is not as uncommon as you would think. If the value of the investment property decreases in the future, then the investor will lose a considerable amount of his money, and the investment will be deemed as a failure. Again, the best way to avoid this risk is to conduct careful research and make a real estate market analysis. Search the state of the economy and learn the chances of economic growth of the real estate market in order to pinpoint the location which has a positive real estate appreciation.

A much easier risk to avoid is legal issues with Airbnb. Airbnb rentals that are short can be a profitable strategy to rent your investment property. However, there have been many cases of local authorities issuing legislation to lessen Airbnb rentals since they have been pressured by local hotels. If this is your investment of choice, you may get in trouble if you follow this real estate strategy in places where Airbnb is illegal. In order to avoid this risk, you could read the city laws that govern the Airbnb rentals to be certain that you are conducting a legal investment.

Investment properties are considered to be relatively safe. However, no real estate investor can be 100% sure that he or she will be successful in making considerable profits out of it. The above risks are some of the most common problems, real estate investors may have to deal with and you should always consider them before you decide to proceed with the purchase of your own investment property. No investment will ever be 100% safe and for this reason, you should be able to plan carefully and take all the necessary measures we mentioned to avoid those common risks.

Smart real estate investors make a thorough real estate market analysis as well as rental property analysis to mitigate those risks. Study the market economy, calculate carefully the expected expenses, and always have a property inspection conducted to your potential investment property. You will not know everything immediately. Most successful real estate investors had to learn everything they know after years of research and experience on the field.

Become a Real Estate Investor from Scratch

To some extent, we can all recognize the most obvious possible financial rewards one could get from investing in real estate. There are many benefits from following this field and the most prevalent one is that a real estate investor will be able to earn a steady source of income to attain financial freedom in the long run. People turn to real estate investing for various reasons. One of them is the fact that they want to quit their boring full-time job and become turn into a real estate investor and save up for their retirement. Don't think that achieving this goal requires for you to have millions set aside. It only takes one rental property to start a real estate business and secure a reliable source of income that comes from renting your property.

By investing in the right locations and making sure that the real estate market along with the housing conditions are moving well together, you can almost be certain that you will be making money out of real estate investing. In other words, if the economy is growing at a steady pace, the housing market will develop too and there will be many real estate opportunities to grasp all over the country. Studying you potential investment property, location, and general condition of the economy will be necessary to secure the perfect investment deal.

Many people are investing in real estate to secure a steady income which comes from rental properties. This form of income is considered to be a passive income and is a major motivator for you to buy your first investment property and start renting it out. Your income out of this could be significant, always depending on the location you choose. Ideally, you will be able to cover your expenses as well as have extra money left. Areas that are almost always high in demand are towns or cities with universities and colleges and those will offer you a higher income through rents.

Keep in mind that no one stops you from investing in more than just one property. You can make the leap and invest in many rental properties to increase and maintain positive cash flow and enrich your investment portfolio. If work becomes too much and you are not able to be everywhere at once you can hire a professional property manager.

Long term financial security is another reason why investors choose to place their money in real estate. You will have a steady income for a long time, especially if you have invested in multiple rental properties. But when you should decide to buy a second investment property to rent? You have to consider several factors before you take this serious step.

The first thing to consider is if you are able to handle another down payment. Even though an investment property typically generates positive cash flow, you will have to make a big down payment. In most cases, this down payment is no less than 20%. For most people, this amount of down payment is not easy and you must consider if you are ready for it.

You have to think of the different ways you will find the money to cover the down payment for the second property you own. If you reach the decision to purchase a second rental investment property, you will have to make sure that you have the necessary cash available for the down payment. In order to avoid financial problems, this is a crucial step. Many lenders check if a real estate investor has reserved cash for several monthly mortgage payments before they give the green light for a loan.

Another thing to consider is making sure you are able to afford the costs of maintenance. Even if you bought your first real estate property to rent it out as an investment or it was your own home, you have probably witnessed how much maintenance a property needs. This will be the case for the second property you think of buying. Even if you renovate the property before renting it out, you will have some unexpected costs that have to do with your tenants and you should also have the financial freedom to repair as well as maintain your properties through vacancies. There is a rule in real estate investing that indicates an investor should have 2% of the sale price of the property set aside in order to cover the annual maintenance costs.

For many investors, the costs of having to maintain one investment property can cause them many problems. For this reason, you should carefully think about how it would be like to maintain two properties. If you are prepared for this task by having 2% of the money you paid for the property set aside specifically for the maintenance of the property, the goal of purchasing a second investment property can be attained.

You should also know how to find an experienced lender to rely on. You may have gone through this process when you decided to purchase your first investment property. If you have not, then you should know that lenders will look for many things such as your financial history, your credit, and your down payment. These things will play an essential part in obtaining a loan. When you decide to ask for a loan to finance your second property, lenders will want to be certain that you will be able to pay back the whole amount of money you owe. Also, lenders will examine your debt-to-income ratio, which essentially is the amount of money you have to pay every month for student loans and generally other bills compared to your income.

It may be more difficult for you to gain the loan you need for your second property since the standards for this case are more difficult to cover. On the other hand, if lenders see that you have managed to pay off your loans on time, they will be more willing to finance your second investment property too. Also, your first investment property will play an important role to help you decide if buying a second one is a good idea.

You should also think about what you wish to do with your second investment property. Building a successful real estate business needs intensive planning. For instance, purchasing a second home to rent out will probably increase your cash flow if you have rented out your first real estate investment property. Do you have a plan for renting out your first property or do you plan on living in it?

If you wish to reside in your first investment property, you will have to pay off the mortgage of this particular property out of your pocket. If you buy a second property in order to rent it out, tenants will help you in paying off your mortgage, but you will have to have the necessary money aside to deal with the various maintenance costs that have to do with your second property. The maintenance costs will depend greatly on whether you want to rent out this second investment property in the long term or for a short time.

Before you decide on whether or not you are able to expand your real estate business plans, you should have a rental strategy. For example, you could rent your property for a short time on Airbnb, but the costs of furniture, repairs, cleaning and other expenses will be on you. Also, you will have to consider whether you want to buy a multi-family property or a single-family property. Buying a second home will help your real estate business grow and if done with the proper rental plan you will be one step closer to achieving financial freedom.

You need to evaluate yourself financially. It is a fact that in order to make money in this field you will need to also spend money. If you wish to start a real estate business from scratch, you will have to start saving up money since there will be a lot of costs involved and considered. For instance, an important expense we have mentioned many times is mortgage and except the 20% down payment, you will have to save up for the monthly mortgage payments.

Doing your homework is also essential for succeeding in real estate. Think of it as going back to school. You will need to learn the basics. For example, knowing who your competitors are is possibly one of the most important things you will have to consider when you are on the hunt for an investment property. How much your competitors charge for rent? What is the vacancy rate of the area you are looking to buy an investment property? How will your investment property be able to compete with others like you? Much like investors, tenants will also conduct their own research when they want to rent a property. They will invest money too in this property by paying rent and residing safely.

Also, it is a fact that nice homes will attract reliable tenants. This is happening because quality tenants will appreciate your place and you need to offer them something they will be proud to use. If the property you want to invest in needs renovations, do not try to save up on expenses by not seeing them through. You don't have to be fancy in order to present quality property. However, quality property is not enough when the location is not appropriate for the tenants you wish to attract. Do not be afraid to research and even go out on your own to ask other residents in the area what is like to live in this neighborhood. It is a small price to pay when compared to the money you may lose due to investing in a bad location.

Also, you should keep in mind that building a successful business especially in real estate is a team game. When the thought of how to start your own real estate business crosses your mind and you start making plans for being successful, you should also think of how to start and maintain a reliable real estate investment network. Starting your business with a reliable team of people that know more things than you do in the early stages of your dream will only improve and ease the steps you will have to make.

You will be asked to do things you have never done before and there will be difficult tasks you never had to deal with before. For this reason, it would be wise if you seek the advice of real estate professionals. This way you will not be solely responsible for every little thing that will present itself to you and as an added bonus you will deal with less stress and headaches. A good start will be for you to find professional property managers, real estate attorneys, handymen, as well as others that will help you in achieving success for your properties.

Last but not least, and possibly the most important step of all the steps you will have to go through, is to be patient. You may not have the smoothest ride when you enter real estate investing, but through hard work and with gaining experience you will be able to earn great amounts of money in almost no time. Just make sure you have money set aside for obtaining good credit and once you are prepared, make your move. Search the internet for investment properties and while you are in the searching process get out and start checking out locations. After you have made your first purchase of investment property, prepare it and rent it out. You have to take your time with real estate and never give up on your goal of building a successful real estate investing business.

Conclusion

As is the case with various things in life, the key to success in real estate is practice and patience. Your daily habits will affect, to a great extent, your chances of becoming a real estate investor since these routines you have or will develop as well as self-discipline will transform your mind, body, and spirit. Develop the habit of waking up early because when you run a business, you will see that there will never be enough time throughout your day to complete every task you have set for that particular day. Take advantage of the power early mornings will give you since they have significant benefits for investors by setting the attitude and tone you will follow for the rest of your day. To quote the word of Ben Franklin:

"Early to bed and early to rise, makes a man healthy, wealthy and wise."

Do you find it useful envisioning your success in order to be motivated and work hard for your goals? Real estate investors have the defining trait of being able to see the big picture. All real estate investors should be able to visualize their success and through this habit create their own success stories. You will change your mentality and develop a new one that will help you set demanding and attainable goals. You will be able to see them through by imagining what you will have and how you will feel when they are complete. What can be a greater motivator for you to realize your dream of being a real estate investor and found your own real estate business?

Understand your weaknesses and strengths. Self-evaluation is extremely important and should be done as early as before you even enter the real estate business. Identify the areas of yourself and your skills that need to be improved and also highlight your top skills. It suffices to say that you should work on those areas of yourself and skillset that you find weak. Being prepared will help you immensely when you enter a new and demanding field that is real estate. Even though you will be able to learn along the way many things, you will never understand through textbooks such as identifying great business deals early on, you will have to make a checklist of what you and your business needs.

As the years pass and you become more experienced you will turn into a real estate entrepreneur. Essentially a real estate investor and a real estate entrepreneur are the same. They are using as an investment real estate in order to generate income, tax benefits, and appreciation. Typically, what separates the two is the fact that a real estate investor is at the beginning of his or her real estate career. An investor has the necessary desire to succeed, but he or she is more focused on daily tasks. A real estate entrepreneur will be able to recognize the bigger picture and know which steps to take to make this picture a reality. In the words of Michael E. Gerber in his book, The E-Myth:

"The Entrepreneur is the visionary in us. The dreamer. The energy behind every human activity. The imagination that sparks the fire of the future. The catalyst for change."

Real estate investing can generate you many profits, profits that will enable you to quit your boring 9-5 job and attain financial freedom. Start saving, research everything you can get your hands on and start working on becoming a successful real estate investor and ultimately a real estate entrepreneur.

Bibliography

1. Ken McElroy: The ABCs of Real Estate Investing: The Secrets of Finding Hidden Profits Most Investors Miss (Rich Dad's Advisors), February 21, 2012.

2. Frank Gallinelli: What Every Real Estate Investor Needs to Know About Cash Flow... And 36 Other Key Financial Measures, Updated Edition, November 18, 2015.

3. Brandon Turner: The Book on Investing in Real Estate with No (and Low) Money Down: Real Life Strategies for Investing in Real Estate Using Other People's Money, August 13, 2014.

4. Brandon Turner and Heather Turner: The Book on Managing Rental Properties: A Proven System for Finding, Screening, and Managing Tenants With Fewer Headaches and Maximum Profit, December 2, 2015.

5. Mark Ferguson: Build a Rental Property Empire: The no-nonsense book on finding

deals, financing the right way, and managing wisely, March 1, 2016.

6. Brandon Turner and Joshua Dorkin: How to Invest in Real Estate: The Ultimate Beginner's Guide to Getting Started, October 31, 2018.

7. David Lindahl: Multi-Family Millions: How Anyone Can Reposition Apartments for Big Profits, April 25, 2008.

8. Ken McElroy: The Advanced Guide to Real Estate Investing: How to Identify the Hottest Markets and Secure the Best Deals (Rich Dad's Advisors, December 10, 2013.

9. Michael Zuber: One Rental At A Time: The Journey to Financial Independence through Real Estate, January 17, 2019.

10. Brian Hennessey: The Due Diligence Handbook For Commercial Real Estate: A Proven System To Save Time, Money, Headaches And Create Value When Buying Commercial Real Estate, June 25, 2015.

11. James A. Randel: Confessions of a Real Estate Entrepreneur: What It Takes To Win

In High-Stakes Commercial Real Estate, January 9, 2006.

12. Than Merrill: The Real Estate Wholesaling Bible: The Fastest, Easiest Way to Get Started in Real Estate Investing, April 14, 2014.

13. Paul Esajian: The Real Estate Rehab Investing Bible: A Proven-Profit System for Finding, Funding, Fixing, and Flipping Houses...Without Lifting a Paintbrush, September 29, 2014.

14. Lisa Phillips: Investing in Rental Properties for Beginners: Buy Low, Rent High, August 13, 2018.

15. Mark Ferguson: Fix and Flip Your Way To Financial Freedom: Finding, Financing, Repairing and Selling Investment Properties. (InvestFourMore Investor Series Book 2), July 28, 2014.

16. Michael E. Gerber: The E-Myth Revisited: Why Most Small Businesses Don't Work and What to Do About It, March 17, 2009.

17. Adam Ovechkin: Passive Income: 40 Ideas to Successfully Launch Your Online Business, 4 Jun 2019.

18. Raza Imam: The Passive Income Playbook: The Simple, Proven, Step-by-Step System You Can Use to Turn Your Expertise Into Passive Income - in the Next 30 Days (Digital Marketing Mastery Book 1), 15 Mar 2019.

19. Mark Atwood: Passive Income: 25 Proven Business Models To Make Money Online From Home (Passive income ideas), 17 Oct 2017.

20. Richard James: Passive Income and Dividend Investing Bundle to Achieve Financial Freedom: The Ultimate Guide to Making Money Online in 2019. Live Anywhere, Escape the 9-5 and Live A Life of Freedom, 30 January 2019.

21. Chris Guillebeau: The $100 Startup: Reinvent the Way You Make a Living, Do What You Love, and Create a New Future, 27 Feb 2018.

22. Brandon R Turner: The Book on Rental Property Investing: How to Create Wealth and Passive Income Through Intelligent Buy & Hold Real Estate Investing!, 2 Dec 2015.

23. Chase Andrews: How to Make $100,000 per Year in Passive Income and Travel the World: The Passive Income Guide to Wealth and Financial Freedom - Features 14 Proven ... and How to Use Them to Make $100K Per Year, 7 Mar 2017.

24. Anthony Johnson: The Ultimate Tutorial for Generating Passive Online Income: Best Ways to Create Online Business and to Start Earning Money Online and From Home, Paperback – 24 Dec 2018.

25. Millionaire Mob: Dividend Investing Your Way to Financial Freedom: A Guide to Live Off Dividends Forever, 5 Nov 2018.

26. Scott Fox: Click Millionaires: Work Less, Live More with an Internet Business You Love, 16 Jun 2012.

27. Michael Ezeanaka: Work From Home: 50 Ways to Make Money Online Analyzed

(Passive Income with Affiliate Marketing, Blogging, Airbnb©, Freelancing, Dropshipping, Ebay, YouTube, ... Etc.) (Business & Money Series Book 3), 8 Aug 2019.

28. Darryl James: 30 Passive Income Ideas: The most trusted passive income guide to taking charge and building your residual income portfolio, 4 Sep 2017.

29. James Ovens: Passive Income Freedom: How to Build Your Financial Wealth and Create Independence! Emulate the Habits of Highly Effective People! Ideas of Business to Retire Early!, 14 Feb 2020.

30. Gundi Gabrielle: Passive Income Freedom: 23 Passive Income Blueprints: Go Step-by-Step from Complete Beginner to $5,000-10,000/mo in the next 6 Months! (Influencer Fast Track® Series), 6 Jan 2019.

31. Mark Morgan: Passive Income 2020: 3 Books in 1 - Complete Beginners Guide on How to Make Money Online by Blogging, eCommerce, Dropshipping, Affiliate Marketing and Amazon FBA, 23 Dec 2019.

Personal Notes

www.ingramcontent.com/pod-product-compliance
Lightning Source LLC
Chambersburg PA
CBHW071555210326
41597CB00019B/3255